A preparatory catechesis for the
World Meeting of Families

Philadelphia, 2015

LOVE IS OUR MISSION

The family fully alive

LOVE IS OUR MISSION

The family fully alive

Copyright © 2014 by World Meeting of Families — Philadelphia. Published 2014

19 18 17 16 15 14   3 4 5 6 7 8 9

ISBN: 978-1-61278-855-5 (Inventory No. T1651)
eISBN: 978-1-61278-866-1
LCCN: 2014945658

Cover design: Tyler Ottinger
Cover art: *Circle of Love* / © 2014 Michael Escoffery / Artists Rights Society (ARS), New York. Photo: Michael Escoffery / Art Resource, NY; *Joachim and Anna,* mosaic by Father Marko Rupnik, 2008 / Chapel of the Holy Spirit at Sacred Heart University, Fairfield, Conn.; *Christ in the House of His Parents,* John Everett Millais, 1863 / Private Collection / Bridgeman Images; *The Holy Family,* Giorgione, c. 1500 / National Gallery of Art, Washington, D.C.
Interior design: Sherri L. Hoffman

PRINTED IN THE UNITED STATES OF AMERICA

PRESENTATION

We are delighted to present this catechesis on family life, as prepared by the Archdiocese of Philadelphia and the Pontifical Council for the Family, in anticipation of the Eighth World Meeting of Families, which will take place in Philadelphia September 22-27, 2015.

This catechesis explains how all of Catholic teaching about sex, marriage, and the family flows from our basic beliefs about Jesus. This catechesis offers a narrative beginning with our creation, soberly noting our fall and the challenges we face, but emphasizing God's plan for our salvation. Love is our mission, and it is by loving God and one another that we will be fully alive.

The Second Vatican Council said that each family is a "domestic church," a small cell of the larger universal Church. This catechesis explores what that means. We encourage everyone to study this catechesis, to discuss it with others, particularly in parishes, and to pray about how the Church can serve families, and how families can serve the Church. The family and the Church are mutually dependent on one another.

In this catechesis, we have tried to present Catholic teaching in a way that is fresh, insightful, and accessible to contemporary Catholics and all people of good will. To paraphrase Saint Augustine, writing in his *Confessions*, God is *ever ancient, ever new*. We hope that this new catechesis confirms for you the beauty and coherence of Catholic teaching, which is sublime and venerable wisdom, and the true source for renewal in every age, including our own.

We look forward to gathering with people from around the world in Philadelphia. As we prepare for this event, we particularly ask the intercessory prayers of Mary and Joseph, parents of the Holy Family and patrons of all families.

Most Reverend Charles J. Chaput, O.F.M. Cap.
Archbishop of Philadelphia

Most Reverend Vincenzo Paglia
President of the Pontifical Council for the Family

LOVE IS OUR MISSION
The family fully alive

Summary statement

The Church believes that God exists and that he loves us. We make this claim because we have encountered and trust Jesus Christ. This trust enables a relationship in which God's plan for all creation is revealed and disclosed. Confident in this plan, we are able to proclaim that each and every human being is created in the image of God. We believe that God creates us with a purpose and for a mission.

We believe that in Jesus, God became man. We believe that in Jesus, God invites and summons the whole world to know him and live as his covenant people in the Church. We believe that God's love is visible and manifest in this covenant, which reveals that God is faithful even unto death, despite our infidelity and sinfulness. We believe that Jesus suffered, died, and rose from the dead, confirming the power and fidelity of God, giving us confidence that his way is true. We trust that as his covenant people, Jesus is now present with us sacramentally, and that ultimately we will share his victory and heavenly communion.

Sustained by the Holy Spirit and the sacraments of the Church, we seek this communion, which Jesus has promised is our destiny. We believe that all aspects of our lives — including our sexuality, fertility, and family life — are part of this mission to live and love as Jesus taught.

We believe that in the Sacrament of Marriage, God has given us the gift of experiencing his covenant. In the marriage covenant, husband and wife live together in light of the covenant already established by God and Israel, Christ and the Church. We believe that marriage is the seedbed of a family, the nucleus of the domestic church, which is itself an essential member of the wider universal Church.

We acknowledge that we are fallen, and that all manner of suffering, temptations, and sins can burden us and prevent us from becoming who we were created to be. But we trust that no matter what trials we face or wounds we inflict upon ourselves and others, God is faithful. His passion, crucifixion, and resurrection are the decisive evidence that he will not depart from his covenant. The Lord has shown that he is stronger than all our sins and that he conquers sin. In our life together, through the presence of Jesus and the Holy Spirit in our midst, we believe that God will bring to fruition the work which he has begun in us. Anticipating that day when Jesus comes again and fully establishes his Kingdom on earth, we believe it is our mission to testify to what God has done and is doing. We believe it is our mission to love God and neighbor as he has taught us.

We believe that love is our mission, and that this mission is the only way we can be fully alive and be who we were created to be. We believe that this love should be taught, shared, and communicated in and through the family, the domestic church. We believe that the family shares in the mission of the whole Church, and we devote this catechesis to explaining this vision of love in more detail.

TABLE OF CONTENTS

The early Church Father Saint Irenaeus famously said that "the glory of God is man fully alive." In like manner, the glory of men and women is their capacity to love as God loves. Life in a family is a summons to embody this love in everyday life.

What Catholics believe about human purpose, marriage, and the family — this is the substance of the following preparatory catechism for the 2015 World Meeting of Families in Philadelphia. This catechesis unfolds in ten steps, or chapters:

We are more than an accident of evolution. We are greater than the sum of our biology. God exists. He is good. He loves us. He made us in his image to share in his joy. He takes an active hand in our lives. He sent his only Son to restore our dignity and lead us home to him.

God works through us. We have a mission. We are in the world for a purpose — to receive God's love and to show God's love to others. God seeks to heal a broken universe. He asks us to be his witnesses and helpers in that work.

The tangible, earthly, corporeal world is more than inert matter or modeling clay for the human will. Creation is sacred. It has sacramental meaning. It reflects God's glory. That includes our bodies. Our sexuality has the power to procreate, and shares in the dignity of being created in the image of God. We need to live accordingly.

We are not made to be alone. Human beings need and complete each other. Friendship and community satisfy that longing with bonds of common interest and love. Marriage is a uniquely intimate form of friendship that calls a man and a woman to love each other in the manner of God's covenant. Marriage is a sacrament. Married love is fruitful and offered without reservation. This love is in the image of Jesus' faithfulness to the Church.

Marriage is meant to be fertile and to welcome new life. Children shape the future, just as they themselves are shaped in their families. Without children, there can be no future. Children reared with love and guidance are the foundation for a loving future. Wounded children portend a wounded future. Families are the bedrock for all larger communities. Families are domestic churches, places where parents help children discover that God loves them and has a plan for each child's life.

Not everyone is called to marriage. But every life is meant to be fertile. Every life has the power and the need to nurture new life — if not through bearing and raising children, then through other vital forms of self-giving, building, and service. The Church is an extended family of different vocations, each distinct but each needing and supporting the others. Priesthood, religious life, and the celibate lay vocation enrich, and are enriched by, the witness of the married state. The different ways of being chaste and celibate outside of marriage are ways of donating one's life to God's service and the human community.

At its best, the family is a school of love, justice, compassion, forgiveness, mutual respect, patience, and humility in the midst of a world darkened by selfishness and conflict. In these ways, the family teaches what it means to be human. However, many temptations arise which try to coax us into forgetting that male and female are created for covenant and communion. For example, poverty, affluence, pornography, contraception, philosophical and other intellectual mistakes can all create contexts that challenge or threaten healthy family life. The Church resists these things for the sake of protecting the family.

Many people, especially today, face painful situations resulting from poverty, disability, illness and addictions, unemployment, and the loneliness of advanced age. But divorce and same-sex attraction impact the life of the family in especially intimate ways. Christian families and networks of families should be sources of mercy, safety, friendship, and support for those struggling with these issues.

The Church has institutional forms because she must work in the world. But that does not exhaust her essence. The Church is the Bride of Christ, a "she," not an "it." In the words of Saint John XXIII, she is our mother and teacher, our comforter and guide, our family of faith. Even when her people and leaders sin, we still need the Church's wisdom, sacraments, support, and proclamation of the truth, because she is the body of Jesus himself in the world — the family of God's people writ large.

God made us for a reason. His love is our life mission. This mission enables us to find our true identity. If we choose to embrace this mission, we will have a new perspective on many issues, not just the family. To live the mission of the domestic church means that Catholic families will sometimes live as minorities, with different values from their surrounding culture. Our mission of love will require courage and fortitude. Jesus is calling, and we can respond, choosing lives of faith, hope, charity, joy, service, and mission.

Man cannot live without love. He remains a being that is incomprehensible for himself, his life is senseless, if love is not revealed to him, if he does not encounter love, if he does not experience it and make it his own, if he does not participate intimately in it. This, as has already been said, is why Christ the Redeemer "fully reveals man to himself." If we may use the expression, this is the human dimension of the mystery of the Redemption. In this dimension, man finds again the greatness, dignity, and value that belong to his humanity.

Pope Saint John Paul II
Redemptor Hominis, 10
March 4, 1979

We will reflect in particular on the family, which is the fundamental cell of society. From the beginning the Creator blessed man and woman so that they might be fruitful and multiply, and so the family then is an image of the Triune God in the world.

Our reflections must keep before us the beauty of the family and marriage, the greatness of this human reality which is so simple and yet so rich, consisting of joys and hopes, of struggles and sufferings, as is the whole of life. We will seek to deepen the theology of the family and discern the pastoral practices which our present situation requires. May we do so thoughtfully and without falling into "casuistry," because this would inevitably diminish the quality of our work. Today, the family is looked down upon and mistreated. We are called to acknowledge how beautiful, true, and good it is to start a family, to be a family today; and how indispensable the family is for the life of the world and for the future of humanity. We are called to make known God's magnificent plan for the family and to help spouses joyfully experience this plan in their lives, as we accompany them amidst so many difficulties.

Pope Francis
Remarks to the Extraordinary Consistory of Cardinals
February 20, 2014

The Creation of Man, Marc Chagall, 1956-58 / © 2014 Artists Rights Society (ARS), New York / ADAGP, Paris. Musee National Message Biblique Marc Chagall, Nice / Peter Willi / Bridgeman Images

I. CREATED FOR JOY

We are more than an accident of evolution. We are greater than the sum of our biology. God exists. He is good. He loves us. He made us in his image to share in his joy. He takes an active hand in our lives. He sent his only Son to restore our dignity and lead us home to him.

A plan for life and the love which sustains us

1. Catholic teaching about marriage and the family flows from the heart of our faith. For this reason, we can begin by reviewing the basic story of the Church. Our God is not inaccessible and remote; we believe that God reveals himself in Jesus Christ. Jesus is the source for the hope, faith, love, and joy that should animate Catholic family life. He is the reason we can trust the wisdom of Catholic belief. Everything we offer in this catechesis flows from Jesus himself.[1]

2. As Pope Francis has recently said of married life, "Promising love for ever is possible when we perceive a plan bigger than our own ideas and undertakings, a plan which sustains us and enables us to surrender our future entirely to the one we love."[2] But we live in a time of deep worldly skepticism about any "bigger plan" or higher meaning to human experience. For many people, the human person is little more than an accident of evolution; carbon atoms with an attitude. In other words, for many people, we have no higher purpose than whatever meaning we create for ourselves.

3. In an era of sophisticated technology and material wealth, that kind of reasoning without God can sound plausible. But in the end, it's too small a vision of who we are as women and men. It undermines human dignity. It leaves starving souls hungry. It is not true.

4. In fact, we yearn for meaning. A longing for purpose is a universal human experience. Thus human beings have always asked basic questions like: "Who am I?" "Why am I here?" "How should I live?" The Christian faith emerged in the ancient Mediterranean mix of Greek, Roman, Hebrew, and other cultures. It was a world where many different answers to life's basic questions struggled for dominance.

5. Our situation today is similar. As in the ancient world, cultures today overlap and penetrate one another. Then as now, philosophies of life compete, offering different visions of what makes a good life. At the same time, suffering and poverty also abound, and so does cynicism — in some cultures — toward any religion or philosophy that claims to offer binding or comprehensive truth.

6. With so many conflicting answers, our age is a confusing time. Many people today honestly seek meaning, but don't know whom to trust or where to commit their lives.

7. Amid this uncertainty, Christians are people who trust in Jesus Christ.[3] Despite the ambiguities of human history, the Catholic way of hope and joy, love and service grounds itself in an encounter with Jesus. As Saint John Paul II proclaimed in his first encyclical: "in man's history, [the] revelation of love and mercy has taken a form and a name: that of Jesus Christ."[4] Everything follows from that. Jesus Christ is the basis of Christian faith.[5]

Jesus reveals God, and the plan begins to unfold

8. In the Bible, Jesus asks his disciples, "Who do you say that I am?" (Mt 16:13-20) Human history for the past 2,000 years has turned on the answer. Christians are people who, having met Jesus in a variety of ways — through the witness of the saints and the apostles, through Scripture and sacrament, in prayer and service to the poor, in worship and through friends and family — are able to trust Jesus, and who say with Peter, "You are the Messiah, the Son of the living God." (Mt 16:16, NRSV)

9. Among many things that he did on earth, Jesus suffered and yet persevered in love; Jesus was crucified by human hands and yet was raised victorious over death. Because God himself suffered these things, Christians believe that God is not remote from the human condition. Nor do we believe in a capricious god, or a deity in competition with human beings. The God in whom we trust wants us to flourish. Because of Jesus Christ, Catholics have confidence in God's love for us. As Pope Francis explained in his first encyclical:

> To those who suffer, God does not provide arguments which explain everything; rather, his response is that of an accompanying presence, a history of goodness which touches every story of suffering and opens up a ray of light. In Christ, God himself wishes to share this path with us and to offer us his gaze so that we might see the light within it. Christ is the one who, having endured suffering, is the "pioneer and perfecter of our faith."[6]

10. In a sense, all of Christian theology is commentary on what it means to say that God became man, died, and rose again. God's presence in human flesh in Jesus means that the transcendent

Creator of the world is also our immanent, intimate, utterly tender Father. The Triune God will always be an infinite mystery, and yet this same God also became a particular man in a particular time and place. God became as vulnerable as a baby in a manger or a man on a cross. Jesus taught and spoke, laughed and wept; his life, death, and resurrection mean that while God is inexhaustibly mysterious, he is not opaque. It is Jesus who enables us to speak about God and divine truth with confidence.

11. Jesus speaks of himself as the Son of the Father, and with his Father sends his Spirit to be with his people. So we learn from him that God's nature is an eternal communion of three divine persons, Father, Son and Holy Spirit. Through baptism into his Church, Jesus invites everyone to be part of God's covenant and to be part of the divine communion. The history of Israel, and later that of the Church, is a history with universal significance, for it is a summons to live as God's people and take part in the divine communion.

Jesus reveals our human identity and destiny

12. Jesus reveals who God is, including that God loves us and reaches out to us. But Jesus also reveals what it means to be human. The Second Vatican Council, speaking of Jesus as the "Word" of God, taught, "The truth is that only in the mystery of the incarnate Word does the mystery of man take on light."[7] In Jesus Christ, we learn things about ourselves that are true, which we could not invent, and which we would not otherwise know. As the Bible puts it, "your life is hidden with Christ." (Col 3:3, NRSV) Catholics believe that God so loves the world (Jn 3:16), that rather than leave us in confusion, God took human flesh to disclose who God is and who we are. The Second Vatican Council explains:

The root reason for human dignity lies in man's call to communion with God. From the very circumstance of his origin, man is already invited to converse with God. For man would not exist were he not created by God's love and constantly preserved by it; and he cannot live fully according to truth unless he freely acknowledges that love and devotes himself to his Creator.[8]

As Pope Benedict XVI stressed at the last World Meeting of Families, in Milan in 2012, "It is love that makes the human person the authentic image of the Blessed Trinity, [the] image of God."[9]

13. The "image of God" phrase comes from Genesis. (Gen 1:26-27, 5:1, and 9:6) It suggests that each individual person is precious, with unique and irreducible dignity. We might abuse or use other people or ourselves, but we cannot erase this truth of how God has created us. Our basic dignity is not contingent on our failures or achievements. The goodness of God and his love for us is prior to, and far more basic than, any human sin. The image of God abides in us, no matter what we do to obscure it. Having been created in the image of God suggests that our true joy and fulfillment lie in knowing, loving, and serving one another as God does.

14. To speak of men and women as the "image of God" means that we cannot speak of humanity without reference to God. If the nature of God is to be a Trinity of communion — Father, Son, and Holy Spirit — and if we are made in that image, then our nature is to be interdependent. To be a person, we need communion.[10] "Being a person in the image and likeness of God thus also involves existing in a relationship, in relation to the other 'I.'"[11] To be ourselves, we need each other, and we need God. We need somebody to love, and

someone to love us. To be who we are created to be, we must give ourselves to our neighbors. "Being a person ... can only be achieved *'through a sincere gift of self.'* The model for this interpretation of the person is God himself as Trinity, as a communion of Persons. To say that man is created in the image and likeness of God means that man is called to exist 'for' others, to become a gift."[12] To save our lives, we must lose them to God. (Mt 10:39, 16:25) This theological account of the human person will become the blueprint for all moral theology, including Catholic teaching about the family.

15. We may dabble in fantasies of self-sufficiency. But we are made in the image of God — and if we want to live as the sons and daughters of God that we truly are, then we must accept God's summons to love God and neighbor. Just as Jesus revealed the nature of God through his love and sacrifice, so too, we accept our real humanity more deeply as we enter into relationships of love and service with our neighbors and in the worship of God.

16. As Vatican II noted in its discussion of human dignity, many atheists believe that "scientific reasoning alone" can tell us all we need to know about ourselves, without reference to anything beyond the natural world.[13] But Catholics hold that theology is essential for anthropology; in other words, we believe that an understanding of God and his purpose for creation is vital to any complete account of human beings. Catholics believe that God's revelation of himself in Jesus gives us back to ourselves, revealing the truth of who we are, disclosing that — most essentially — we belong to God. God's love is basic to our identity, and more fundamental than any anxieties, ambitions, or questions we may have. As Saint John Paul II taught early in his pontificate, "The man who wishes to understand himself thoroughly — and not just in accordance with immediate, partial,

often superficial, and even illusory standards and measures of his being — he must with his unrest, uncertainty and even his weakness and sinfulness, with his life and death, draw near to Christ."[14]

17. When teaching about marriage, Jesus himself refers to God's plan and purpose in creation. When the Pharisees challenge Jesus with a question about divorce, his answer recalls that God created human beings male and female, and that husband and wife become one flesh.[15] (Mt 19:3-12, Mk 10:2-12) Similarly, when the Apostle Paul writes to the Corinthians about sexual ethics, he reminds them of the one flesh union of man and woman in creation. (1 Cor 6:16) When he writes to the Ephesians about marriage, he again reminds them of that union, and tells them that it is a "profound mystery" which refers to Christ and the Church. (Eph 5:32) Writing to the Church in Rome, he speaks of God's nature and will being revealed in creation, and speaks of the many sins — including sexual sins — that arise from turning away from our knowledge of the creator. (Rom 1:18-32)

Love is the family mission

18. By now it should be clear why "Love is our mission" is the theme for the 2015 World Meeting of Families. One of the most significant 20th-century papal documents on family life — *Familiaris Consortio*, again by Saint John Paul II — summarized how Catholic teaching about God and human nature shapes Catholic beliefs about how we should live:

> God created man in his own image and likeness: calling him to existence through love, he called him at the same time for love. God is love and in himself he lives a mystery of personal loving communion. Creating the human race in

his own image and continually keeping it in being, God inscribed in the humanity of man and woman the vocation, and thus the capacity and responsibility, of love and communion. Love is therefore the fundamental and innate vocation of every human being.[16]

God's love never ceases to summon us. We cannot forfeit this invitation. We have been created in the image of God, and despite the reality of human sin, the vocation implicit in our creation can never be erased.

19. Catholic views on marriage, family, and sexuality belong to a larger mission to live in a way that makes God's love visible and radiant; to live this mission makes everyday life alive with God's joy. The entire human person — body and soul, our maleness and femaleness, and all that follows from each — is implicated in God's invitation. The subtitle for this World Meeting of Families is "the family fully alive," and for good reason. The family is most fully alive when we embrace God's invitation to be the sons and daughters he created us to be.

20. *Our era is a confusing and uncertain time. Jesus Christ is a trustworthy anchor. Human dignity rests securely in Jesus, God become man. Jesus reveals who God is, and who we are. In Jesus, we meet a God who reaches out to us, who creates communion and invites us to share in his joy. We are made in God's image and called to communion with him and each other. This love gives purpose and shape to all aspects of human life, including the family.*

QUESTIONS FOR DISCUSSION ————————————

a) What is it about Jesus that makes him trustworthy?

b) What things in your life distract you from Jesus? What would help you to become more familiar or even intimate with him?

c) What does it mean to be "created in the image of God"? Is it possible to understand human identity without God? Why or why not?

d) "Love is our mission" is the theme of this catechesis. What does "love" mean in your life? How might a mission to love affect your choices, priorities, and ambitions?

The Holy Family / © Vie de Jesus Mafa / www.jesusmafa.com

II. THE MISSION OF LOVE

God works through us. We have a mission. We are in the world for a purpose — to receive God's love ourselves and to show God's love to others. God seeks to heal a broken universe. He asks us to be his witnesses and helpers in that work.

Scripture gives content and shape to the meaning of love

21. With men and women created in the image of God, history begins. In history, God calls and forms a people. He makes a covenant with us, first through Israel and then through Christ and the Church. In this relationship, God teaches us to love as he loves.

22. In other words, having been created for communion, we learn that love is our mission. The gift of our existence precedes and shapes what we do and how we live. In short, "God's way of loving becomes the measure of human love."[17]

23. To live this way requires humility. It requires us to conform our hearts to God and see the world through his eyes. God's way is a better way, but not always the easier way.

24. The Bible bursts with imagery of God's love. God is a father welcoming home his prodigal son and hosting a feast. (Lk 15:11-32) God is a shepherd searching for his lost sheep. (Lk 15:3-7) God is a

mother who comforts her children. (Isa 66:13) God is a friend who lays down his life for others, and who weeps when his friends suffer. (Jn 11:35) God is a teacher, leading us to love and serve one another as neighbors. (Mt 22:39) God is a gardener, tending us until we bear good fruit. (Jn 15:1) God is a king inviting us to his son's wedding banquet. (Mt 22:1-14) God hears a blind man's cry, and stops to ask: what do you want me to do for you? (Mk 10:46-52) God is welcoming, filled with compassion for his people when they are hungry, offering them food (Mt 14:13-21),[18] and offering himself. (Mt 26:26)

Marriage is an essential biblical image for God's love

25. All these images and many others help us see the depths of God's love. They highlight the kind of love we are called to witness in our own lives. But, as Pope Benedict XVI observed, one key image gives us a context for all the others:

"God loves his people." Indeed, biblical revelation is above all an expression of a love story, the story of God's covenant with humankind. This is why the story of the union of life and love between a man and a woman in the covenant of marriage was used by God as a symbol of salvation history.[19]

26. Marriage imagery is central in describing God's covenant with Israel and, later, his covenant with the Church. As Pope Benedict XVI taught, "Marriage based on exclusive and definitive love becomes the icon of the relationship between God and his people and vice versa."[20] God's covenant is a central theme of Scripture, and marriage is the Bible's privileged metaphor for describing God's relationship with humanity. Along these lines, when he was still Archbishop of Munich, Pope Benedict XVI had explained:

We can say that God created the universe in order to enter into a history of love with humankind. He created it so that love could exist. Behind this lie words of Israel that lead directly to the New Testament.... God created the universe in order to be able to become a human being and pour out his love upon us and to invite us to love him in return.[21]

27. This marital imagery begins in the Old Testament. Here we learn that God loves us intimately, with tenderness and longing. "The Prophets, particularly Hosea and Ezekiel, described God's passion for his people using boldly erotic images."[22] In Hosea, God promises to "allure" Israel, speaking "tenderly to her," until she will "respond as in the days of her youth" and call me "my husband." (Hos 2:14-16) In Ezekiel, God speaks to Israel in sensuous imagery: "I spread the edge of my cloak over you, and covered your nakedness; I pledged myself to you and entered into a covenant with you, says the Lord God, and you became mine. Then I bathed you with water ... and anointed you with oil.... You grew exceptionally beautiful, fit to be a queen."[23] (Ezek 16:8-13, NRSV) We find similar language in Isaiah,[24] Jeremiah,[25] and the Psalms.[26] The Song of Songs has also sparked centuries of sermons using marriage to explain the intensity of God's love for his people.

The Bible is not sentimental about marital love

28. The marriage between God and his people can be rocky. "God's relationship with Israel is described using the metaphors of betrothal and marriage," so when God's people sin, our waywardness becomes a kind of "adultery and prostitution."[27] In Hosea, God's love for Israel puts him in the position of a betrayed husband with a faithless bride. As God says to Hosea, "Go, love a woman who has a

lover and is an adulteress, just as the Lord loves the people of Israel, though they turn to other gods." (Hos 3:1, NRSV)

29. When the people of God forget his commands, neglect the poor in their midst, seek security from alien powers, or turn to false gods — then adultery and prostitution are exactly the right words for their infidelity.[28]

30. Yet God remains steadfast. Reflecting recently on Ezekiel 16, Pope Francis noted how God speaks words of love even when Israel is unfaithful.[29] Israel sins. Israel forgets. Israel prostitutes herself, pursuing false gods. But God will not abandon his covenant people. Repentance and forgiveness are always possible. God's mercy means that he seeks Israel's good even as she flees him. "For the Lord has called you like a wife forsaken and grieved in spirit, like the wife of a man's youth when she is cast off, says your God. For a brief moment I abandoned you, but with great compassion I will gather you ... with everlasting love I will have compassion on you." (Isa 54:6-8, NRSV) God perseveres in love for his people, even when we fall, even when we insist on trying to live without him.

31. In like manner, Christian love involves much more than emotion. It includes the erotic and affective, but it is also a choice. Love is a mission that we receive, a disposition that we accept, a summons to which we submit. This kind of love has dimensions we discover as we yield to it. This kind of love seeks and follows God, whose covenant fidelity teaches what love is. God never discards Israel for a more appealing partner. Nor is he deterred by rejection. He is never fickle. He wills only the best, the true and ultimate good for his people. And while his love for Israel is passionate with desire — no one reading the prophets can deny that — this "erotic" aspect to

divine love is always leavened with God's sacrificial fidelity.[30] God's *eros* always integrates with his compassion and patience.

Marriage, love, and Christ's sacrifice on the cross

32. God's love is captured vividly in Ephesians 5, where Saint Paul extends the marriage analogy to Christ and the Church.[31] Paul urges both husbands and wives to "be subject to one another out of reverence for Christ." (Eph 5:21, NRSV) Christian marriage is therefore not a negotiation over rights and responsibilities, but rather a description of mutual self-giving. It is far more radical than mere egalitarianism. Paul does write that "the husband is the head of the wife just as Christ is the head of the church." (Eph 5:23, NRSV) But what does this mean in context and in practice? Paul calls husbands to a self-giving love that mirrors Christ's sacrifice on the cross. Undermining machismo and exploitation, and in profound contrast to other household codes in the ancient world, Paul teaches a dynamic in the image of God: "husbands, love your wives, just as Christ loved the church and gave himself up for her." (Eph 5:25, NRSV) Drawing on Ephesians 5, the Church speaks of marriage as a sacrament, and summons couples to this kind of cruciform self-sacrificial communion.

33. Jesus enables Christians to speak confidently about God's love. He opens up God's covenant to all people, completing Israel's history as a universal narrative of redemption. Jesus embodies life-giving love because he is, literally, God's Word made flesh. He loves the Church as his bride, and this unselfish love — proven in blood on the cross — sets the model for the kind of mutual love and service needed within every Christian marriage and family.

34. As Pope Benedict XVI taught: "By contemplating the pierced side of Christ, we can understand ... God is love. It is there that this truth can be contemplated. It is from there that our definition of love must begin. In this contemplation the Christian discovers the path along which his life and love must move."[32]

35. For many today, "love" is little more than a warm feeling or physical attraction. These things have their place. But real love — love that endures and deepens and satisfies the human heart over a lifetime — grows from what we give to others, not what we take for ourselves. The Lord Jesus Christ died on a cross for our salvation. That kind of radical, liberating capacity to abandon our prerogatives and give ourselves to others is the thread that unites all Catholic teaching on marriage and the family. Authentic Catholic teaching on marriage and the family separates true love from all counterfeits.

36. *Scripture has many complementary and overlapping ways of describing God's love, but marriage is foremost among them. The covenant between God and his people — first Israel and then the Church — is like a marriage. This marriage is not always easy, but human sin never has the last word. God's fidelity reveals what true love and fidelity look like. Jesus Christ, who welcomes all of us into membership in God's family, gives us a new and unexpected definition of love, giving us new possibilities for living.*

QUESTIONS FOR DISCUSSION

a) Why is God's love like a marriage?

b) How is God's way of loving different from our human way of loving?

c) What is true love and how do we recognize it? What are some similarities and differences between your culture's notion of romantic love and God's covenant love?

d) Can you think of a time when God's love helped you to love in a more honest and better way?

The Creation, God Introducing Adam and Eve, Jean Fouquet, c. 1470 / Bibliotheque Nationale, Paris, France / Bridgeman Images

III. THE MEANING OF HUMAN SEXUALITY

The tangible, earthly, corporeal world is more than inert matter or modeling clay for the human will. Creation is sacred. It has sacramental meaning. It reflects God's glory. That includes our bodies. Our sexuality has the power to procreate, and shares in the dignity of being created in the image of God. We need to live accordingly.

The natural physical world bursts with spiritual goodness

37. The Catholic faith has always been a robustly "physical" religion. The Bible begins in a garden and ends with a feast.[33] God made the world, called it good, and entered into its history. Jesus Christ, God's Son, took flesh and became one of us. In the sacraments, material things are consecrated and made visible signs of grace. Ordinary bread and wine, water, oil, and the touch of human hands are all tangible ways in which God's presence becomes effective and real.

38. We believe in the corporal works of mercy. When we feed the hungry, give drink to the thirsty, clothe the naked, shelter the homeless, attend to the sick, visit the imprisoned, or bury the dead, we actually minister to Jesus. (Mt 25:25-40) We trust in the goodness of God's creation. (Gen 1:4-31) This confidence permeates the Catholic imagination. It becomes visible in our art and architecture,

our liturgical calendar's rhythm of feasting and fasting, and our folk pieties and sacramentals.

Male and female sexuality participate in our spiritual purpose

39. Material creation has spiritual meaning, which has implications for the way we live as male and female. Our sexuality has purpose. Our bodies are not simply shells for the soul or sensory machines for the brain. Nor are they raw material we can freely abuse or reprogram. For Christians, body and spirit are profoundly integrated. Each human being is a unity of body and soul. Saint Hildegard of Bingen wrote, "The body is, in truth, the temple of the soul, cooperating with the soul by means of the senses, as a mill wheel is turned by water."[34] The body has innate dignity as part of God's creation. It is an intimate part of our identity and our eternal destiny. The two sexes literally enflesh God's design for human interdependence, community, and openness to new life. We cannot debase or abuse the body without inflicting a cost on the spirit.

40. Of course, we do not always love as we ought. Sex is a uniquely powerful factor in human affairs — both for good and for ill. And so sexuality misused or disordered has always been a major source of confusion and sin. Sexual desire and self-understanding can be complex. Our identity is revealed in Jesus and in God's plan for our lives, and not in fallen self-assertions.

41. Marriage exists because procreation and communion, biology and God's covenant, nature and super-nature, together undergird what it means to be "human." Marriage exists because we discover and accept, rather than invent or renegotiate, the vocation to self-giving which is intrinsic to being created male and female under the

covenant. Marriage is God's creation because we are God's creatures, and because God created male and female for fellowship with him in his covenant.

42. Our origin as two different and complementary sexes, and our call to love, to communion, and to life,[35] are one and the same moment. In the words of Pope Francis: "This is the story of love. This is the story of the masterpiece of creation."[36]

43. This call to love, communion, and life involves the entire being of man and woman, body and soul. The human person is simultaneously a physical and spiritual being.[37] The body, in a sense, reveals the person.[38] As a result, human sexuality is never merely functional. Sexual difference, visible in the body, contributes directly to the body's spousal character and the person's capacity to love.[39] At the center of this call to love is God's summons to "be fruitful and multiply." (Gen 1:28, NRSV) A couple's spousal union through the body is therefore, by its very nature, also a call to live as father and mother.[40]

44. For good reason, we hear delight in Adam's words at his first sight of Eve: "This at last is bone of my bones and flesh of my flesh." (Gen 2:23, NRSV) The *Catechism of the Catholic Church* notes that, from the beginning, "man discovers woman as another 'I,' sharing the same humanity."[41] Man and woman share an equal dignity that comes from God their Creator. In God's plan, both the similarity and otherness of man and woman coincide in their sexual complementarity as masculine and feminine. Created together (Gen 1:26-27), man and woman are willed *for* each other.[42] Sexual difference is a primordial reminder that we are made to give ourselves away to others guided by virtue and God's love.

45. Saint John Paul II often spoke about the "nuptial or spousal meaning of the body."[43] He echoed the teaching of Vatican II that the "partnership of man and woman constitutes the first form of communion between persons."[44] But sexual difference marks all our relationships, even for the unmarried, since we each enter life as a son or a daughter. We are called to be a brother or sister not only to those in our families, but also to the needy in our neighborhoods, communities, and churches. Our identity as men and women is the basis of our call to fatherhood or motherhood, natural or spiritual. In this way, sexual difference has universal significance.

46. Because it is a central component of our identity, sexuality cannot be isolated from the meaning of the human person. Sex is never simply a physical or emotional impulse. It always involves more. Sexual desire shows that we are never self-sufficient. We long for intimacy with another. Sexual intercourse, no matter how "casual," is never simply a biological act. In fact, sexual intimacy is always in some sense conjugal because it creates a human bond, no matter how unintended. A properly ordered conjugal act is never simply an inward looking, autonomous erotic act. Our sexuality is personal and intimate, but always with a social dimension and consequence. A sacramental marriage is never a private possession, but discovers itself in relation to God's wider covenant.

We have sexual ethics because sex has spiritual significance

47. Two different vocations do justice to the summons of being male and female in God's plan: marriage and celibacy. Both of these disciplines converge on the shared premise that sexual intimacy between a man and woman belongs and flourishes in the context of a covenant. Celibacy is the way that unmarried people confirm the truth and beauty of marriage. Celibacy and marriage both abstain

from sexual acts that use others in conditional or temporary ways. Authentic celibate abstinence is certainly not a disdain for sex, but rather honors sex by insisting that sexual intimacy serves and is served by the covenant. By living in the light of the covenant, married couples and celibate persons alike offer their sexuality to the community, to the creation of a society which is not premised on concupiscence and exploitation.

48. The next three chapters will speak in more detail about marriage (Chapters 4 and 5) and celibacy (Chapter 6). But both ways of living are grounded in God's summons to live masculinity and femininity in generous, self-giving ways. Both ways of living look to God's covenant and receive the fact of being created as male and female as occasions for joy. The discipline we impose on our love — the discipline of the covenant — is sometimes felt as a burden. But precisely this discipline honors and reveals the true meaning of love created in the image of God.

49. Our creation as men and women in the image of God is why we are all called to the virtue of chastity. Chastity is expressed in different ways, according to whether or not we are married. But for everyone, chastity involves refusing to use our own or other people's bodies as objects for consumption. Chastity is the habit, whether we are married or not, of living our sexuality with dignity and grace in the light of God's commandments. Lust is the opposite of chastity. Lust involves looking at others in utilitarian ways, as if the other's body existed merely to satisfy an appetite. True chastity "does not disdain the body" but sees the body in the full dimensions of personhood.[45] Chastity is a great "yes" to the truth of humanity created in the image of God and called to live in the covenant.

50. Understood this way, chastity is something everyone is called to practice. "All the baptized are called to chastity.... Married people are called to live conjugal chastity; others practice chastity in continence."[46] Chaste married love situates *eros* in the context of love, care, fidelity, and openness to children. Chaste celibacy, through its continence, concurs that sexual intimacy belongs in the context of love, care, and fidelity.

51. The roots of this Christian teaching are ancient. As Saint Ambrose wrote in the fourth century: "There are three forms of the virtue of chastity: the first is that of spouses, the second that of widows, and the third that of virgins. We do not praise any of them to the exclusion of others.... This is what makes for the richness of the discipline of the Church."[47]

52. How to live this teaching concretely through either marriage or celibacy and in today's sometimes difficult circumstances — that task will guide us in remainder of this catechesis.

53. *God created the whole material world out of his love for us. Everything we can see and touch, including our male and female bodies, was created for the sake of God's covenant. We do not always love as we ought, but God's pattern of love protects us and calls us back to our true natures. Marriage and celibacy are the two ways of being together as male or female in light of God's covenant, and for this reason both marriage and celibacy are considered chaste ways of living.*

QUESTIONS FOR DISCUSSION ————————

a) Why do Catholics enjoy and value the physical, tangible world so much? Think of anything beautiful, such as nature, bodies, food, or art — why are these things so important in Catholic tradition?

b) What is the purpose of creation? Is the physical world a blank slate, which we're free to rule and exploit according to our own desires?

c) Things like rest, food, pleasure, and beauty are attractive. But sometimes we have deeply felt desires and appetites beyond what is good for us. How do we know when a desire is legitimate and good? How can we cherish and enjoy creation and our bodies in daily life?

d) Why do you think Catholic practice traditionally includes both feasting and fasting? Celibacy and marriage?

Joachim and Anna, mosaic by Father Marko Rupnik, 2008 / Chapel of the Holy Spirit at Sacred Heart University, Fairfield, Conn.

IV. TWO BECOME ONE

We are not made to be alone. Human beings need and complete each other. Friendship and community satisfy that longing with bonds of common interest and love. Marriage is a uniquely intimate form of friendship that calls a man and a woman to love each other in the manner of God's covenant. Marriage is a Sacrament. Married love is fruitful and offered without reservation. This love is in the image of Jesus' faithfulness to the Church.

Virtue, love, and goodness help fulfill our destiny

54. 1 Corinthians 13:4-7 is a popular Scripture choice for Christian weddings: "Love is patient; love is kind; love is not envious or boastful or arrogant or rude. It does not insist on its own way; it is not irritable or resentful; it does not rejoice in wrongdoing, but rejoices in the truth. It bears all things, believes all things, hopes all things, endures all things." (NRSV)

55. The text is beautiful. Having been created in the image of God, loving this way coheres with our true human nature. But loving this way is never easy. It demands humility and patience. As Pope Francis recently said, "Faith is no refuge for the fainthearted."[48] Marital love must be built on more than romance. Romance is wonderful — but alone, it can't survive the cares and challenges that inevitably visit every married couple. To be what we are — to love as we were created to love — certain virtues are necessary. We must be alive to these virtues, and cultivate them, in order to fulfill our destiny.

41

56. Saint John Paul II's "Theology of the Body" speaks of a certain "interior freedom" and "self-mastery" which spouses need in order to truly make a gift of themselves to one another.[49] A person tied too tightly to romantic expectations, without the leaven of interior freedom and the capacity for self-gift, will lack flexibility. To live the sacramentality of marriage and to follow the way of the covenant, husbands and wives need the capacity to transcend resentment, to lay aside entitlements, and to step forward in generosity. Without this interior freedom and power, serious problems are bound to arise, because life puts husbands and wives in situations that are very often not romantic at all.

57. No marriage founded on mere sexual chemistry endures. Erotic partners focused mainly on possessing each other lack the interior skill of stepping back and making space for self-criticism, reconciliation, and growth. The marital promise to love steadfastly as God does helps to create and protect this vital space. The sacramental commitment to do the work of love, even when loving is tough, is an essential ingredient in God's covenant.

Genuine love makes a commitment

58. No mortal can satisfy all our longings. Real marital unity is based on God's covenant, a covenant which welcomes erotic desire, but which even more fundamentally commits men and women to each other in sickness and in health, for richer or poorer. Christian marriage is not a romantic audition or a conditional arrangement "until further notice."[50] A so-called trial marriage, an attempt to live intimately but hypothetically, to test the relationship and pursue it as long as the romance is flowing, is a contradiction in terms.[51] Pope Francis recently made this point in a public address:

> But you both know that marriage is for life? "Ah, we love
> each other so much, but ... we'll stay together as long as the

love lasts. When it ends, we'll each go our separate way." This is selfishness: When I feel like it, I'll end the marriage and forget the "one flesh" that cannot be separated. It is risky to get married: it is risky! It is this egoism which threatens it, because we each have within us this possibility of a dual personality: The one that says, "I am free, I want this ..." and the other which says, "I, me, to me, with me, for me...." Selfishness always returns and does not know how to open up to others.[52]

In a postmodern world where trust is scarce, marriage seems daunting. We worry that we may be tied to someone wrong. In a globalized world, where economic anxiety is often well-founded, we may also worry that all of life's challenges and questions, about financial or economic security, must be answered and put to rest before we can love as Jesus did.

59. In response to the range of possible worries and fears, the Church offers Jesus, the sacraments, and the support of her own members in mutual fellowship, confident that for all its challenges the Christian way of loving is possible and will reveal our true selves. The Church promises her sons and daughters that marriage is a sacrament, that the bond and practice of Catholic marriage makes sustaining grace real, present, and efficacious. In response to our fears and anxieties, the Church insists that to promise love in the manner of the covenant is not a hypothetical for mythical saints who are perfect, but a real and possible commitment for actual sinners who are on the way. As Pope Francis puts it: "The Sacrament of Marriage ... takes place in the simplicity and also the fragility of the human condition. We know the many trials and difficulties that the lives of a married couple encounter.... The important thing is to keep alive the link with God, which is the basis of the marital bond."[53]

60. To love in this way is not something we postpone, saying we will try once we have put to rest certain practical questions; rather, life's practical questions are adequately approached only when we love in this way. To love in this way is not an ideal on an ever-receding horizon; rather, to love in this way is something that we choose to do in everyday life, beginning here and now amidst daily pressures. As Pope Francis taught on another occasion:

> Matrimony is [a] work of every day; I could say a craftwork, a goldsmith's work, because the husband has the task to make his wife more woman, and the wife has the task to make her husband more man. To grow also in humanity, as man and as woman. And this is done between you. It is called growing together. This doesn't come from the air! The Lord blesses it, but it comes from your hands, from your attitudes, from your way of living, from your way of loving one another. Make yourselves grow! Always act so that the other grows.[54]

Pope Francis acknowledges that many people might be afraid of such a challenge; that people might avoid marriage out of skepticism or fear:

> Today many people are afraid of making definitive decisions, that affect them for all their lives, because it seems impossible ... and this mentality leads many who are preparing for marriage to say, "We will stay together for as long as our love lasts." But what do we mean by "love"? A mere emotion, a psycho-physical state? Certainly, if it is just this, it cannot provide the foundation for building something solid. But if instead love is a relationship, then it is a growing reality, and we can also say, by way of example, that it is

built in the same way that we build a house. And we build a house together, not alone! ... You would not wish to build it on the shifting sands of emotions, but on the rock of true love, the love that comes from God.... We must not allow ourselves to be conquered by a "throwaway culture." This fear of "forever" is cured by entrusting oneself day by day to the Lord Jesus in a life that becomes a daily spiritual path of common growth, step by step.[55]

Good marriages are built on virtues, especially mercy and chastity

61. People who want to build their marriage on rock will cultivate certain virtues. The *Catechism of the Catholic Church* promises that in the Sacrament of Marriage, Christ dwells with a couple, helping spouses to pick up their cross, "to rise again after they have fallen," to forgive and bear one another's burdens.[56] Pope Francis makes a related point succinctly when he says living together is an "art ... which can be summarized in [a few simple] words: please, thank you, and sorry."[57] Learning to say these things can be hard. But marriages can turn very painful, very fast, when these simple words are missing.

62. All of the cardinal virtues (prudence, temperance, justice, fortitude) and theological virtues (faith, hope, and love) are necessary and relevant for marriage to flourish. Chastity in particular is the seed from which strong marriages grow. To train our hearts for marriage, we need practice in interior freedom, the practice of seeing our sexuality in the context of communion and the holiness of each other's personhood. Chastity forms the good habits of self-denial and self-control, which are prerequisites for treating others with mercy. Marriage fantasies, absent a chaste heart, make a poor start for a long walk of mercy.

63. Real marital unity also relies on mercy, a quality we learn from Jesus and see throughout God's covenant. In the Liturgy, we pray "Lord have mercy." Jesus gives us his mercy so we can be merciful.

64. Mercy grows when we love as Christ showed us. The "grace of Christian marriage is a fruit of Christ's cross, the source of all Christian life."[58] Catholics believe that "Christ himself is at work" in each of the seven sacraments, and that the Holy Spirit is a fire in the sacraments, transforming into the divine life whatever it touches.[59] In the Sacrament of Marriage, God's covenant is made visible, the covenant's grace is communicated and shared.[60] In the Sacrament of Marriage, God's covenant enters our homes and becomes the foundations of our families.

65. Christian marriage is a matter of mutual self-surrender. And of course there are alternatives, other models of marriage on offer in society at large. But to the degree that "marriage" is a prize we allow ourselves and a partner only after a long sequence of erotic auditions, or to the extent that "marriage" is a contract, a division of rights between individuals protecting their own autonomy, then we are sowing the seeds of disappointment and conflict. *Eros* will wax and wane, and a framework of contesting rights is not fertile ground for mercy.

66. Over the centuries, human beings have married for countless reasons, some of them ennobling, some of them pragmatic. In sacramental marriage, the Church offers us shelter, grace, and a daily lesson in the nature of God's love. The Church's marital vows constantly recall a husband and wife to their better natures, and situate a marriage in relation to the other sacraments as well, especially Penance and Eucharist. This sacramental economy puts reconciliation and fidelity at the foundation of married life, and, in so doing,

fosters and protects true communion between the sexes. To people in postmodern times, uncertain what and who can be trusted, such a venture seems risky. But the Church, a mother who knows the human heart better than we know ourselves, also knows who Jesus is, that he is the Lord, that he is trustworthy — and that his way of loving is, in the end, the only way.

67. Jesus creates a new possibility for us, a vision of marriage based on his covenant with the Church, a marriage based on abiding permanence, chastity, and mercy. We can see how this sacramental marriage integrates with the whole of Christian life, for cultivating the virtues of love, interior freedom, fidelity, mercy, and forgiveness is a lifelong project which builds upon habits of prayer, participation in the Sacraments, and familiarity with the story of God's covenant. The Lord knows that no marriage displays all the virtues all the time, but in his mercy, he gives us Penance and Eucharist so that we might grow in our capacity to love as Jesus does. Orienting our lives this way demands sacrifice, but in the end, this life is beautiful. Jesus is the path of truth and joy.

QUESTIONS FOR DISCUSSION ————————————

a) What is the Catholic spirituality of marriage? What can families do to celebrate and protect Christian marriage?

b) If marriage is a sacrament, what are the implications for courtship? What qualities should we seek in a potential spouse?

c) How do the Sacraments of Penance and Eucharist relate to the Sacrament of Marriage?

d) In the Lord's Prayer, we say, "forgive us our trespasses as we forgive those who trespass against us." Do you find it easy or difficult to do that? How does forgiveness enable relationships?

The Holy Family, Giorgione, c. 1500 / National Gallery of Art, Washington, D.C.

V. CREATING THE FUTURE

Marriage is meant to be fertile and to welcome new life. Children shape the future, just as they themselves are shaped in their families. Without children, there can be no future. Children reared with love and guidance are the foundation for a loving future. Wounded children portend a wounded future. Families are the bedrock for all larger communities. Families are domestic churches, places where parents help children discover that God loves them and has a plan for each child's life.

Marriage gives spiritual context to the possibilities created by biology

68. Marriage includes love, loyalty, and commitment. But so do many other worthy relationships. Marriage is something distinct. Marriage is the covenant built on the procreative power of male and female. Our biology poses certain limits and possibilities, and marriage is one answer for living this situation in holiness.

69. We will treat the other answer — celibacy — in the next chapter. We will discuss challenges to the idea of fertility in marriage, challenges which arise from the questions of contraceptive marriage and same-sex relationships, in Chapter 7. In this section, we need to discuss how married love integrates the fertility of men and women with the sacrament of God's covenant.

70. Marriage is a response to the possibility of procreation between men and women. When a man and a woman marry by taking the additional step of freely consenting to mutual promises of fidelity and permanence,[61] marriage places procreation in the context of human dignity and freedom. The marital vows are analogous to God's covenant with Israel and the Church. Marriage, as the Church teaches, is "the matrimonial covenant, by which a man and a woman establish between themselves a partnership of the whole of life and which is ordered by its nature to the good of the spouses and the procreation and education of offspring, has been raised by Christ the Lord to the dignity of a sacrament between the baptized."[62] In short, marriage is a community of both life and love.[63]

71. The Sacrament of Marriage makes the power of God's covenant fidelity, as well as his Triune communion as Father, Son, and Holy Spirit, available to a husband and a wife. This spiritual foundation gives a new and deeper rationale for biological fecundity, for welcoming children is an extension of divine generosity. In this way, we can see how the classic Augustinian "three goods of marriage" (children, fidelity, and sacrament) are all rooted in the divine plan.[64]

The spiritual vocation of parenting

72. As with any vocational question, the question of whether and when to have children is not something to decide simply according to self-focused human criteria. There are real and legitimate human "physical, economic, psychological, and social conditions" which husbands and wives should consider in their discernment.[65] But, in the end, the question of becoming parents rests on the same rationale as sacramental marriage itself: love in the shape of service, sacrifice, trust, and openness to God's generosity. Catholic marriage is premised on the sacraments and the support of Christian community,

and so, when Catholic spouses consider becoming Catholic parents, they continue in this same spiritual and community context.

73. When spouses become parents, the inner dynamic of God's creation and the marriage sacrament is made visible in a beautiful and particularly clear way. When a husband and wife have children after the pattern of Christ's love for us, this same love also orients the new parents to their children's education and spiritual formation.[66] "These children are links in a chain," said Pope Francis when he recently baptized 32 babies. "You parents have a baby son or daughter to be baptized, but, in several years, it will be they that have a baby to baptize or a grandchild; and so, the chain of faith!"[67]

74. This chain of children and parenting spans millennia. Twice a day — and still today — Jewish prayers open with the ancient *Sh'ma*, a prayer found in Deuteronomy:

> Hear O Israel, the LORD our God, the LORD is one. You shall love the LORD your God with all your heart, and with all your soul, and with all your might. Keep these words that I am commanding you today in your heart. *Recite them to your children* and talk about them when you are at home and when you are away, when you lie down and when you rise.[68]

75. We repeat: *Recite them to your children.* At the heart of this command, this foundational responsibility, is the daily reaffirmation of the covenant between God and Israel. Parents should nurture and usher children into their community's relationship with God. Thus Deuteronomy says: Recite and share the glories of God with your children. Jesus says the same thing to his disciples: Let them come unto me. (Mt 19:14) Both Deuteronomy and Jesus are speaking to us. Both of them are saying: *Make sure the children in your care have*

*a relationship with God and the people of God. Teach children to pray
and contemplate the Lord. Nurture this daily in your home, and do not
create obstacles to it.*

76. This vocation gives purpose to Catholic parenting. The same
love that sweeps up men and women, teaching them the ways of the
covenant and bringing them to the Sacrament of Marriage, leads a
couple to become a family.[69] A husband and wife become a father
and mother: "From the wedlock of Christians there comes the family, in which new citizens of human society are born, who by the
grace of the Holy Spirit received in baptism are made children of
God, thus perpetuating the people of God through the centuries."[70]
Christians have children not merely to continue the species and
build up society, but that the whole family might be formed for the
communion of saints. In the words of Saint Augustine, the sexual
love of male and female "is the seedbed, as it were, of a city,"[71] and
he has in mind not only the earthly city or civil society, but also the
heavenly city, the Church come to full flower.

Life in the domestic church

77. Vatican II called the family a "domestic church," an *Ecclesia domestica*:

> The family is, so to speak, the domestic church. In it parents
> should, by their word and example, be the first preachers of
> the faith to their children; they should encourage them in
> the vocation which is proper to each of them, fostering with
> special care vocation to a sacred state.[72]

The vocational nature of family life requires living with attentiveness.
"Every human life is called to some task by God,"[73] but, like building
a marriage, discerning a vocation does not "come from the air."[74] The

habits of discernment can be taught and cultivated. It is a mother's and a father's responsibility to be with children at home and in church and pray together regularly. They will not learn how to do it if they are not taught. Parents can seek help from godparents, grandparents, teachers, clergy, and religious to help fulfill their responsibilities and so that they too can grow and learn about prayer. Pope Francis, a Jesuit with years of formation in the art of discernment, describes how prayer and vocational awareness go together: "It is important to have a daily relationship with [God], to listen to him in silence before the Tabernacle and deep within ourselves, to speak with him, to draw near to the sacraments. Having this familiar relationship with the Lord is like keeping the window of our lives open so that he can make us hear his voice and hear what he wants us to do."[75]

78. Practicing and teaching discernment as a family imply patience and prayer, a constant desire to purify motives, to confess and do penance, to be patient in the slow work of growing in virtue, to open one's imagination to Scripture and the witness of the Church, and to understand one's inner life. To learn discernment for ourselves and to pass it along to our children are tasks that imply humility, an openness to constructive criticism, and conversation about how God might be at work in our life. A vocational approach to life implies a willingness to be frank about our own desires, but, most of all, to offer our life to God, to be open to the adventures and new plans that might present themselves when we say "thy will, not mine."[76] Saint Thérèse of Lisieux prayed in this way as a child, saying: "My God, I choose all. I do not want to be a saint by halves. I am not afraid to suffer for you. I fear only one thing — that I should keep my own will. So take it, for I choose all that you will."[77]

79. Especially when a family includes many young children, parents face a wide array of stresses. Parenting is demanding. Yet if

the goal of Christian family life is to open the home's windows to God's grace in daily life, then even in the midst of fatigue and domestic chaos, parents can remain open to the Spirit. Nobody wants to burden parents further. But "divine love ... is not something to be reserved for important matters, but must be pursued chiefly in the ordinary circumstances of life."[78] In the vulnerability of such moments, parents can discover what Saint Paul meant when he said "whenever I am weak, then I am strong." (2 Cor 12:10, NRSV)

80. Parenting has a way of deflating pretenses; of making us see that we are not self-sufficient but need help and strength from God, family, parish, and friends. The way a family responds to adversity and sickness, or gathers for meals and devotions, or makes financial decisions and sets priorities, or the way a family makes choices about leisure, the parents' jobs or careers, the children's academic education, even bedtime routines — these and many other daily aspects of "home economics" shape the imaginations and horizons of the children. Domestic routines can be "thin places," places where the Spirit shines through, where an attitude of gentleness and Christian hospitality leavens all of life.

Our cultural context requires families to be discerning

81. Pope Francis expresses many of these ideas in a practical way:

> I think we can all improve a bit in this respect: by becoming better listeners of the Word of God, in order to be less rich on our own words and richer in his words.... I think of fathers and mothers, who are the primary educators [of their children]: how can they educate them if their consciences have not been enlightened by the Word of God? If their way of thinking and acting is not guided by the Word, what sort of example can they possibly give to their children? This is

important, because then mothers and fathers complain: "Oh, this child..." But you, what witness have you given the child? How have you spoken to him? Have you talked with him about the Word of God or about TV news? Fathers and mothers need to be talking about the Word of God! And I think of catechists and of all those who are involved in education: if their hearts have not been warmed by the Word, how can they warm the hearts of others, of children, of youth, of adults? It is not enough just to read the Sacred Scriptures, we need to listen to Jesus who speaks in them: it is Jesus himself who speaks in the Scriptures, it is Jesus who speaks in them.... Let us ask ourselves ... what place does the Word of God have in my life, in my everyday life? Am I tuned into God or into the many buzz words or into myself? This is a question that everyone of us needs to ask him- or herself.[79]

82. Pope Francis alluded to the TV news, which we may take more generally as raising the issue of mass media, Internet social media, and other forms of popular culture. Engaging these forms of culture is not something that should happen on autopilot; to engage these forms of culture constructively also requires discernment. The *Catechism of the Catholic Church*, in discussing the domestic church, notes that the world today is "often alien and even hostile to faith."[80] In a fragmented culture, where the social and media environment may undermine parental authority in general, and Catholic parenting in particular, parents and children need to reflect on their family's way of being in the world without belonging to the world.[81]

83. When any of us — but especially children — encounter culture, it shapes our imaginations and ambitions. In large part, all of us — but especially children — learn our expectations for a good life in part from the images, films, music, and stories in our lives. It is therefore

up to parents, the extended family, godparents, adult mentors, and educators to monitor this exposure, and to ensure children's imaginations are fortified and fed with wholesome food, with material that protects their innocence, gives them an appetite for the adventure of Christian living, and evokes a vocational approach to life. Beauty and contemplation should be part of a child's ordinary environment so that children can learn to perceive the sacramental dimension to reality. Parents, elders, godparents, relatives, fellow parishioners, catechists, and teachers need to model these attitudes for children. The formation of young people necessarily includes "book knowledge." Spiritual literacy means knowing the facts of the faith. But it is even more vital to teach children how to pray, and to give children role models, adult examples for them to witness and aspire toward.

84. Older children and adolescents can become appropriately self-conscious and reflective about the ambient culture, as well as beginning to form a more mature perspective on prayer and vocational discernment. These important themes should be part of preparing to receive the Sacrament of Confirmation, which itself gives grace to enable faithful discipleship on these questions.[82]

The family and the parish depend upon each other

85. The *Ecclesia domestica* cannot exist, of course, without the *Ecclesia*. The domestic church implies a relationship to the universal Church: "The family, to be a 'little Church,' must be well integrated into the 'big Church,' that is, into the family of God that Christ came to form."[83] Regular participation in Sunday Mass with the universal Church is a *sine qua non* for the domestic church to fulfill its name. The universal Church is the bearer and teacher of God's covenant with his people, the same covenant which enables and sustains married and family life.

86. Pope Benedict XVI spoke of the parish as a "family of families" which is "able to share with each other, not only the joys but the inevitable difficulties of initiating family life."[84] Certainly sacraments, and very often the corporal works of mercy, can be helpfully facilitated by the parish. Children need to see their parents and other adults in their lives demonstrating solidarity with the poor and doing things which serve the poor. Parishes and dioceses can help provide these occasions.[85] The domestic church serves the parish and is served by the parish.

87. The parish, the diocese, and other Catholic institutions such as schools, movements, and associations, are especially key for children who do not have two parents. Children may be without one or both parents for a variety of reasons, including death and illness, divorce, immigration, war, alcohol and drug addictions, domestic violence, abuse, political persecution, and unemployment or itinerant working conditions due to poverty.[86] Sadly, sometimes husbands and wives and mothers and fathers separate, often for reasons demanding our compassion. "The emotional upheaval suffered by children of separated couples who suddenly find themselves with a single parent or in a 'new' family poses a challenge for bishops, catechists, teachers, and all who are responsible for the young.... It is not a question of replacing their parents but of collaborating with them."[87]

88. For a parish to actually be a "family of families" calls for concrete actions of hospitality and generosity. Saint John Paul II said that "opening the door of one's home, and still more of one's heart," is a mode of imitating Christ.[88] To give help and to receive help are intimate things. No one, especially a child, parents struggling with unexpected crises, vulnerable elderly people, or anyone who is suffering, should be lonely in a parish family. There is no substitute for ordinary parishioners simply befriending and serving one another

during the week, extending church beyond Sunday mornings. How lay people treat each other will determine whether a parish is fulfilling its mission in this way. This vision of parish life *must be taught* and modeled by clergy, perhaps especially in large parishes where there can be a temptation to anonymity. But, in the end, to make a parish alive in this way cannot be clericalised. This is a vision of church life that requires lay people. Saint Paul told the people in Galatia that if you "bear one another's burdens," then you "will fulfill the law of Christ." (Gal 6:2, NRSV) By implication, then, if we are not bearing one another's burdens, if we are leaving vulnerable families and single people to fend for themselves in loneliness, then we are selling ourselves short. If our lifestyles are not based on communion and service, then we cannot flourish. We were made for one another, and to live as if that is not true is a sadness, a failure to fulfill the life-giving law of Christ.

89. Hospitality to lonely children will naturally raise the question of adoption. John Paul II, speaking to a convocation of adoptive families, said:

> To adopt a child is a great *work of love*. When it is done, much is given, but much is also received. It is a true exchange of gifts.
>
> In this area, unfortunately, our time knows many contradictions. Despite the numerous children who, because of the death or inability of their parents, are left without a family, there are so many couples who decide to have no children for often selfish reasons. Others let themselves be discouraged by economic, social, or bureaucratic difficulties. Still others, in the desire to have their "own" child at any cost, go far beyond the legitimate help which medical science can offer procreation, even having recourse to mor-

ally reprehensible practices. Regarding these tendencies, it must be said that the norms of moral law are more than mere abstract principles, but safeguard the true good of man, and in this case, the good of the child with respect to the interests of his parents.[89]

John Paul II hoped that "Christian families will be able to show greater readiness to adopt and foster children who have lost their parents or have been abandoned by them."[90] He could venture this hope because the love that animates a Christian marriage is God's covenant, a love which is eternally hospitable and filled with life.

90. *Sexual intimacy between men and women raises the possibility of children. No other relationship carries this basic, organic, biological possibility. Marriage between a man and a woman brings this potential fertility into a spiritual context. Parenting is a spiritual vocation, for it ultimately means preparing our children to be saints. This bold ambition entails humble but important practices in the home, such as prayer and cultivating a spiritual disposition. It requires parents to be discerning about how a family engages in the wider culture. Introducing children to the Lord means that a domestic church will want to integrate with the parish as well as the wider universal Church. The challenges of family life require support — no family can flourish on its own. To flourish, families need their parishes, and their parishes need them. Lay people are needed to create and serve in these ministries.*

QUESTIONS FOR DISCUSSION

a) How does the marriage of a man and a woman differ from other close friendships?

b) Have you ever prayed with a child? How about reading the Bible with a child, or discussing some other aspect of the faith? If you are not a parent yourself, are there children in your life who could use a friend and mentor?

c) What are the habits of discernment? What does a vocational approach to life look like?

d) What is a domestic church? How does the parish serve the family, and how does the family serve the parish? How can a family and a parish "fulfill the law of Christ" as described in Galatians 6:2?

Washing of the Feet / © 2000 by John August Swanson / Serigraph 21 by 26 / www.JohnAugustSwanson.com

VI. ALL LOVE BEARS FRUIT

Not everyone is called to marriage. But every life is meant to be fertile. Every life has the power and the need to nurture new life — if not through bearing and raising children, then through other vital forms of self-giving, building, and service. The Church is an extended family of different vocations, each distinct but each needing and supporting the others. Priesthood, religious life, and the celibate lay vocation enrich, and are enriched by, the witness of the married state. The different ways of being chaste and celibate outside of marriage are ways of donating one's life to God's service and the human community.

The spiritual fertility of celibacy

91. Two of the Church's sacraments are unique in that they are both devoted "to the salvation of others." Both Holy Orders and Marriage "confer a special grace for a particular mission in the Church to serve and build up the people of God."[91]

92. In other words, not all men and women need to be biological parents to radiate God's love or take part in the "family of families" we know as the Church. The vocation to the priesthood, or vowed religious life, has its own integrity and glory. The Church always needs priests and religious, and parents must help all their sons and daughters listen for the possibility that God might be calling them to offer their lives in this way.

93. Furthermore, there are many celibate lay people, with their own irreplaceable role in the Church. The Church fosters many distinct ways of practicing celibacy, but all of them are, one way or another, a call to serve the Church and foster communion in ways that are analogous with parenting.

94. Authentic celibacy — whether lay, ordained, or vowed — is oriented toward social and community life. To be a "spiritual father" or "spiritual mother" — perhaps as a member of the clergy or religious, but also as a godparent, or an adopted relative, or a catechist or teacher, or simply as a mentor and friend — is an esteemed vocation, something essential for a healthy and flourishing Christian community.

95. Saint John Paul II once reflected on the maternal qualities of Mother Teresa, and, by extension, the fruitfulness and spiritual fertility of celibate life more generally:

> It is not unusual to call a religious "mother." But this name had special intensity for Mother Teresa. A mother is recognized by her ability to give herself. Seeing Mother Teresa's manner, attitudes, way of being, helps us understand what it meant to her, beyond the purely physical dimension, to be a mother; it helped her to go to the spiritual root of motherhood.
>
> We certainly know what her secret was: she was filled with Christ, and therefore looked at everyone with the eyes and heart of Christ. She had taken seriously his words: "I was hungry and you gave me food…" She therefore had no trouble in "adopting" her poor as children.
>
> Her love was concrete and enterprising: it spurred her to go where few had the courage to go, wherever poverty was so great as to be frightening.

It is not surprising that the people of our time were fascinated by her. She incarnated that love which Jesus indicated as the distinctive mark of his disciples: "By this all men will know that you are my disciples, if you have love for one another."[92]

Radiant lives, like Blessed Teresa of Calcutta and Saint John Paul II, show that celibacy in its many varieties can be a compelling, beautiful way of life.

The rationale and possibilities of celibacy

96. Earlier in this catechesis, citing Saint Augustine, we saw that the purpose of having children was not merely to continue the species or build up civil society, but to fill the heavenly city with the joy of new life. This distinction — between the natural goal of procreation and the theological vocation to prepare for the Kingdom of God in full flower — enables the Church to make a further point: To fulfill their destiny as men and women, all persons can be fruitful, but not everyone need marry.

97. The Church offers marriage as a vocation, a possibility; it therefore cannot be a law or requirement for a flourishing Catholic life.[93] It follows, then, that celibacy needs to exist in the Church's social life in order for marriage to be a matter of freedom rather than compulsion. Celibacy is the alternative if there is indeed more than one way to order one's sexual life, one's maleness or femaleness, to heaven. "Family life is the vocation that God inscribed into the nature of man and woman, and there is another vocation which is complementary to marriage: the call to celibacy and virginity for the sake of the Kingdom of Heaven. It is the vocation that Jesus himself lived."[94]

65

98. Celibacy and marriage do not compete with one another. Again, as Saint Ambrose taught: "We do not praise any one of them to the exclusion of others.... This is what makes for the richness of the discipline of the Church."[95] Celibacy and marriage are complementary vocations because they both proclaim that sexual intimacy cannot be an audition.[96] Both celibates and married persons respect the structure of covenant love and avoid "trial" or conditional intimacy.[97] Both celibacy and marriage reject sex in the context of what Pope Francis called the "throwaway culture."[98] Both celibacy and marriage reject sexual relationships premised merely on satisfying erotic desire.

99. Observing the disciplines of celibacy and marriage are the two ways for men and women to be in solidarity with one another without sexual exploitation. Celibacy and marriage are the *only* two ways of life which converge on the conclusion that marriage is the fully human form for procreative acts in light of God's design which abides in us and shapes our lives. Celibacy — which includes not only priests and vowed religious, but all those who are chaste outside of marriage — is the way of life for people who are not married but who honor covenants.

100. Everything the Church has taught about being created for joy, about being created in the image of God, about needing to love and be loved, applies equally to celibate and married persons. Celibacy can be confirmed and permanent, as in vowed religious life, or someone unable to marry due to disability or circumstance, or only potentially permanent, as in a young person discerning a vocation. In all of these cases, celibacy follows in the footsteps of Jesus, flourishing by offering the self to God and trusting his plan, and building a life premised on loving others with mercy, patience, generosity, and service.

101. In any society, many will be marginalized if marriage is seen as mandatory, as if one needs a romantic partner in order to be complete. Celibacy in the Church rebels against this misleading idea. For example, widows are often cast aside in traditional societies, and single people in modern cities often socialize in clubs, pubs, and bars where promiscuity is normal. To create alternative space, where people who are not married can experience joy and have a mission, is a profound hospitality, something Christians need to do for one another as a form of liberation and welcome.

102. Some people, due to circumstances beyond their control, will want to marry, but will not be able to find a spouse. A life of hope and waiting does not mean abandonment to a sterile existence. When living in active readiness for God's will as it unfolds in one's own personal history, making Mary's fiat one's own,[99] blessings can accrue. Because everyone is called to give and receive love, because Christian love is outward looking, celibacy is a communal practice. When we love one another chastely outside of marriage, the fruit is friendship: "The virtue of chastity blossoms in *friendship.... Chastity is expressed notably in *friendship with one's neighbor*. Whether it develops between persons of the same or opposite sex, friendship represents a great good for all. It leads to spiritual communion."[100]

103. Celibates — and to a limited but somewhat analogous extent, infertile couples — also enjoy a unique freedom, an attractive liberty for certain types of service, friendship, and community. Celibates and the childless are relatively more available for chaste experiments in community living, for careers which demand flexibility, for prayer and contemplation. Celibates, couples without children, and even healthy elderly people (perhaps with grown children) have gifts of time in ways which parents typically do not. Such people can entertain catechetical work and other parish ministries,

or even apostolates and witness in dangerous situations that would be impossible for families with children. The unmarried or otherwise childless enjoy an availability which gives them somewhat more discretion and creativity about the possibilities for hospitality and friendship. When Saint Paul counsels celibacy, he thinks he is offering a possibility which has its challenges, but it also has its benefits and freedoms: "But if you marry, you do not sin, and if a virgin marries, she does not sin. Yet those who marry will experience distress in this life, and I would spare you that…. I want you to be free from anxieties." (1 Cor 7:28-32a, NRSV)

The spiritual and social alliance between celibacy and marriage

104. The *Catechism of the Catholic Church* says: "All Christ's faithful are called to lead a chaste life in keeping with their particular states of life. At the moment of his Baptism, the Christian is pledged to lead his affective life in chastity."[101] Celibacy is therefore allied to marriage, making a similar interior offering of our whole self to the Lord. Both celibate people and married people pledge their lives to God's covenant according to their respective vocations. There are practical differences in every particular individual's vocation, but the internal motion of soul, the heart's offering of itself, is similar at its core. Wise, mature celibates and spouses are familiar with many of the same spiritual skills.

105. In the case of marriage, when husbands and wives give themselves to one another, with a love that imitates Jesus, their gift of self to each other is part of the work of Christ, joining in the same spirit of Jesus' own gift of himself for the Church. When the spouses exchange their vows in church at their wedding liturgy, Christ receives their nuptial love and makes it part of his own Eucharistic gift of self for the Church and the Father who, pleased by the offering of

the Son, gives the Holy Spirit to the spouses to seal their union.[102] Nuptial fruitfulness, then, is first of all the gift and the task of the sacramental bond. This is exactly why Saint John Paul II beautifully said that the nuptial bond that the spouses have been given to enjoy and live makes them "the permanent reminder to the Church of what happened on the Cross; they are for one another and for the children witnesses to the salvation in which the sacrament makes them sharers."[103]

106. In the case of celibacy, similar reasoning is at work. Christ's love is continent because he makes a total gift of himself, an unconditional affirmation of the other: "What shall a man give in return for his life?" (Mt 16:26) Christ's love is expressed in his desire to share all of himself with his disciples (Lk 22:15), to give himself to them fully in order to bring everyone back to the Father to share God's own glory.[104] Marital love is the covenant's rationale shaping how we procreate; celibate love is the covenant's rationale brought to life in the whole community.

107. Since marriage and celibacy are complementary vocations for adult Catholics, we should raise our young people to see that a romantic partner is not essential for human happiness. If marriage itself takes shape from Jesus' covenant with us, and if that same covenant makes celibacy a viable alternative as well, then the life of young people who are not married is better understood, not so much in terms of courtship or "dating," but as a time of discernment and cultivating friendships. The habits and skills of true friendship are basic to either life in marriage or celibate community. The question about vocation which faces adolescents and other young people today needs to involve more than romantic preference. Young people need to acquire certain internal spiritual skills regardless of what their future life holds.

108. For this reason, parishes should pay careful attention to the social dimension of chastity and celibacy. Celibacy imposes unique challenges, and, as the *Catechism of the Catholic Church* observes, learning sexual self-mastery has a cultural aspect: we are interdependent persons, and practicing chastity is either helped or hindered by our social situation.[105] The possibilities for life which young people find imaginable depend on the examples they see and the stories they hear.

109. Because celibacy is so countercultural, a risk exists even in parishes that it might not be fully understood. Single persons "deserve the special affection and active solicitude of the Church, especially of pastors."[106] Not only pastors, but also families and single people themselves, should take concrete steps to ensure that "single" in a Catholic context is clearly not the same as being lonely or isolated. Single people need fellowship for sharing their burdens and sorrows, as well as accountability and opportunities for service. "The doors of homes, the 'domestic churches,' and of the great family which is the Church must be open" to the unmarried.[107]

110. This vision suggests a need for everyone to examine how they contribute to the atmosphere and substance of parish life. If parents discourage children from the priesthood, vowed religious life, or other celibate vocations, then the entire community should examine its conscience. Authentic celibacy is always richly social, and if celibacy is seen as uniquely lonely or alienated, then something in the practice or structure of community life has gone awry. Celibates should take initiatives to serve and involve themselves, and families should take steps to be hospitable, to adopt "aunts" and "uncles," and to be inclusive in building extended households or intentional communities.

111. A rich social life makes all types of celibacy much more plausible to the world, for it undermines the critique of celibacy that says such a life is inevitably lonely. To live this vision, to overcome the inertia of social habits that segregate singles and overlook the opportunities of celibacy, demands creative commitment from lay and clergy alike. Jesus is our Lord, and the Lord says, "Everyone will know that you are my disciples, if you have love for another." (Jn 13:35, NRSV) Love should visibly animate parish life for everyone.

112. *Celibacy is not sterile, nor is it "single" in the sense of isolated or autonomous. In the Church, we are all interdependent, created for communion, created to give and receive love. This vision of human life generates an inexhaustible variety of creative vocations. Celibacy places unique demands on those who embrace it, but celibates also have unique privileges and opportunities. Celibates respect the sexual or biological potential of marriage, and operate from a similar rationale and spirituality of self-giving. Celibates and married couples need one another to sustain and grow the "family of families" that is called Church.*

QUESTIONS FOR DISCUSSION ————————

a) What do celibacy and marriage have in common?

b) What are some of the trials or burdens that unmarried people face in your community? How can friends, families, and parishes help? What are some of the benefits of celibacy? How can unmarried people serve the community?

c) Do the children in your parish get to meet a wide range of priests, monks, friars, nuns, and other religious sisters? Can you think of ways to introduce examples of celibacy into your community?

Have you ever encouraged the children you know to become a priest or vowed religious? Why or why not?

d) What are some good reasons for choosing either marriage or celibacy? What are some not-so-good reasons? How should a person discern his or her vocation?

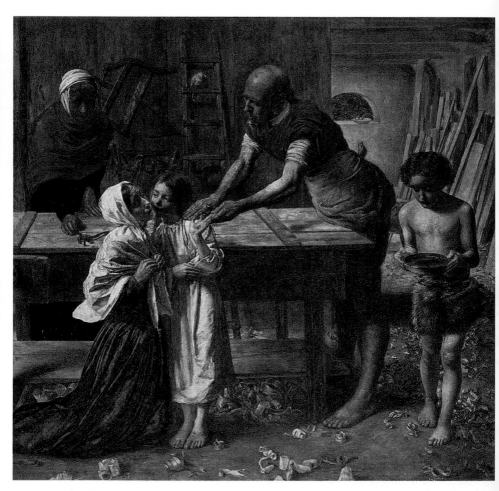

Christ in the House of His Parents, John Everett Millais, 1863 / Private Collection / Bridgeman Images

VII. LIGHT IN A DARK WORLD

At its best, the family is a school of love, justice, compassion, forgiveness, mutual respect, patience, and humility in the midst of a world darkened by selfishness and conflict. In these ways, the family teaches what it means to be human. However, many temptations arise which try to coax us into forgetting that male and female are created for covenant and communion. For example, poverty, affluence, pornography, contraception, philosophical and other intellectual mistakes can all create contexts that challenge or threaten healthy family life. The Church resists these things for the sake of protecting the family.

The effects of the fall

113. We are fallen creatures. We do not always love as we ought. But if we own and name our sins, we can repent of them.

114. We can see proof of the fall in our everyday actions: in our divided hearts, and in the obstacles to virtue so common in the world. The "regime of sin" makes itself "felt in the relationships between man and woman. Their union has always been threatened by discord, a spirit of domination, infidelity, jealousy, and conflicts that can escalate into hatred and separation. This disorder can manifest itself more or less acutely, and can be more or less overcome according to the circumstances of cultures, era, and individuals, but it does seem to have a universal character."[108]

115. The Preparatory Document for the 2014 Extraordinary Synod of Bishops on "Pastoral Challenges to the Family in the Context of Evangelization" mentions a vast number of global issues:

> The many new situations requiring the Church's attention and pastoral care include: mixed or interreligious marriages; the single-parent family; polygamy; marriages with the consequent problem of a dowry, sometimes understood as the purchase price of the woman; the caste system; a culture of non-commitment and a presumption that the marriage bond can be temporary; forms of feminism hostile to the Church; migration and the reformulation of the very concept of the family; relativist pluralism in the conception of marriage; the influence of the media on popular culture in its understanding of marriage and family life; underlying trends of thought in legislative proposals which devalue the idea of permanence and faithfulness in the marriage covenant; an increase in the practice of surrogate motherhood (*wombs for hire*); and new interpretations of what is considered a human right.[109]

Economic issues and contexts

116. Poverty and economic hardship undermine marriage and family life around the world. Pointing to a sign in the crowd one day at an Angelus in St. Peter's Square, Pope Francis said:

> I read there, in large print: "The poor cannot wait." It is beautiful! And this makes me think of Jesus born in a stable, he was not born in a home. Afterwards he had to flee, to go to Egypt to save his life. Then he returned to his home in Nazareth. And I think today, also in reading what is written there, of the many families who do not have a home,

either because they never had one or because they lost it for any number of reasons. Family and home go together. It is very difficult to bring up a family without living in a house.... I invite everyone — persons, social institutions, authorities — to do everything possible so that every family might have a home.[110]

117. At the same time, social-science data show that stable marriages and families help to *overcome* poverty, just as poverty works *against* stable marriages and families. Strong marriages and families create hope, and hope leads to purpose and achievement. This fact suggests one way a vigorous Christian faith has practical as well as spiritual consequences. Helping families to break vicious cycles, and transform them into virtuous cycles, is one reason the Church pays attention to the economic circumstances of our lives as well as the spiritual ones.

118. Pope Benedict XVI's last encyclical, *Caritas in Veritate*, insists on "the strong links between life ethics and social ethics."[111] Benedict observed that "the family needs to have a home, employment and a just recognition of the domestic activity of parents, the possibility of schooling for children, and basic health care for all."[112] Jesus Christ cares for the whole person; he himself was no stranger to poverty and came from a family who were once refugees;[113] he now calls his Church to stand in solidarity with families in similar situations.[114]

119. In other words, if we say we care about the family, we need to care for the poor. If we care for the poor, we will be serving families.

120. Today's global hyper-capitalist economy also damages the middle classes and the affluent. For example, mass culture commodifies

sex. Corporate marketing creates an endless appetite for new experiences, a climate of perpetually roaming and unsatisfied desire. Life in modern market cultures becomes a struggle against the cacophony of distraction, noise, and restless hungers, all of which disrupt family stability and fuel a sense of entitlement. Life in a perpetual marketplace may tempt us to think that if we desire something, if it is consensual and we can afford it financially, then we are entitled to it. That sense of entitlement is a destructive illusion, a type of slavery to the appetites, diminishing our freedom for living virtuously. Our failure to embrace limits, our stubborn insistence on our appetites, fuels many spiritual and material problems in our world today.

Why pornography and masturbation are wrong

121. Commodifying sex always entails commodifying persons. Pornography — often linked to and fed by the cruelty of human trafficking — is now pandemic, not just among men, but increasingly among women. This lucrative global industry can invade any home with a computer or cable television. Pornography catechizes its consumers in selfishness, teaching its users to see other people as objects to satisfy our appetites.

122. For each of us, the task of learning patience, generosity, forbearance, magnanimity, and other aspects of cruciform love is difficult enough. Pornography makes giving ourselves to other people and to God's covenant even harder, even for the casual user. Masturbation is wrong for analogous reasons. When a person "enjoys" or rationalizes using pornography or resorting to masturbation, he or she leeches away the capacity for self-denial, mature sexuality, and genuine intimacy with a spouse. It's little wonder that pornography plays a large role in many of today's broken marriages. Pornography and masturbation can also attack the vocation of celibate persons precisely because they can seem so private.

Why contraception is wrong

123. In like manner, contraception also leads us to see sexual desire as an entitlement. It enables users to treat the desire for sexual intimacy as self-justifying. By separating procreation from communion, contraception obscures and ultimately undermines the rationale for marriage.

124. Married couples who contracept might do so with good intentions. Many married couples experience and believe that their contraceptive sex is essential for holding their marriage together, or that contraceptive sex is harmless and victimless. Many married couples have become so habituated to contraception that the Church's teaching can seem shocking.

125. But if a married couple are indeed seeking the interior freedom, mutual self-giving, and self-sacrificial love to which God's covenant summons us all, then it is hard to imagine in what sense contraception is necessary and essential. The Church believes that insistence on contraception rests upon myths about marriage which are not true. As Pope Pius XII explained:

> There are some who would allege that happiness in marriage is in direct proportion to the reciprocal enjoyment in conjugal relations. It is not so: indeed, happiness in marriage is in direct proportion to the mutual respect of the partners, even in their intimate relations.[115]

126. In other words, to regard contraception as necessary or even helpful works from a confused premise. At its roots, a happy marriage — the kind that endures over a lifetime — has more in common with the generous, patient, self-giving powers of celibacy than what Pius XII called "a refined hedonism."[116] Recently, Pope Francis

referred to the Holy Family in highlighting the qualities of generosity and interior freedom that enable a good marriage:

> Joseph was a man who always listened to the voice of God, he was deeply sensitive to his secret will, he was a man attentive to the messages that came to him from the depths of his heart and from on high. He did not persist in following his own plan for his life, he did not allow bitterness to poison his soul; rather, he was ready to make himself available to the news that, in a such a bewildering way, was being presented to him. And thus, he was a good man. He did not hate, and he did not allow bitterness to poison his soul.... And Joseph thereby became even freer and greater. By accepting himself according to God's design, Joseph fully finds himself, beyond himself. His freedom to renounce even what is his … and his full interior availability to the will of God challenges us and shows us the way.[117]

127. Contraception obscures this interior freedom and power. To the extent sexual desires are treated as entitlements, or desires that can never be postponed, the need to grow in interior freedom is revealed. As a "technical solution" to what is actually a moral problem, contraception "conceals the basic question that concerns the meaning of human sexuality and the need for a responsible mastery of it so that its practice may become an expression of personal love."[118]

The benefits of natural family planning

128. Certainly "responsible parenthood" includes discerning when to have children. Serious reasons, arising from "physical, economic, psychological, and social conditions," can lead a husband and a wife to "decide not to have additional children for either a certain or indefinite period of time."[119]

129. Catholic husbands and wives who find themselves in this situation need teachers, mentors, and friends who can train and support them in natural family planning (NFP). Parishes and dioceses should make this help a pastoral priority and easy to find. It is profoundly more likely that a couple will actually live Catholic teaching if they have spiritual direction, practical instruction, and supportive friends. Lay people, pastors, and bishops all have responsibilities for creating these enabling conditions.

130. If a married couple, with generous hearts and after genuine prayer and reflection, discern that it is not a season in life when God is calling them to have additional children, then from time to time, NFP will require them to abstain from sexual relations. Practicing NFP in this way, the spouses subordinate or offer their short-term sexual desires to their larger sense of God's call upon their lives. This subordination of will and desire is one of the many ways in which NFP and contraception are so different from each other, both objectively and experientially. NFP is an intimate and demanding, and therefore potentially beautiful and deepening, path of following the Lord in marriage.

131. NFP is premised upon the beauty and necessity of marital sexual intimacy. Because it also relies on occasional abstinence for the sake of spacing births, NFP summons couples to communication and self-mastery. Like the marriage bond itself, NFP shapes and disciplines sexual desire. The very idea of monogamy presupposes that fallen sexual men and women can patiently discipline otherwise roaming desires, and learn to treat a spouse with generosity and fidelity. In this way, the periodic abstinence required by NFP works to deepen and explore a commitment that married people have already made. NFP does not guarantee a happy marriage, nor does it exempt a marriage from all the ordinary sufferings of

marriage, but NFP is an attempt to build a household on rock and not sand.

Contraception spreads confusion about marriage more widely in society

132. As the Church predicted nearly 50 years ago, contraception not only undermines marriages, but has other harmful side effects in society as well.[120] Ubiquitous contraception means that few are in the habit of abstinence and sexual self-control. In this way, contraception has made celibacy much less plausible to modern people and thereby made marriage or other types of romantic coupling seem virtually inevitable. When that happens, all of a community's social life is distorted. And insofar as contraception drains celibacy of its plausibility, it contributes to the shortage of young priests and vowed religious. Contraception also makes sex outside of marriage (whether premarital or extramarital) appear superficially more plausible, as if sexual intimacy could exist without consequences. And, of course, many of the same arguments for childless sex that seek to justify contraception apply just as well, but with even uglier and more brutal results, to permissive abortion.

133. In separating sex and procreation, contraception encourages a culture to premise marriage on emotional and erotic companionship. This reductionist, disordered view feeds much of today's confusion about what marriage really is, making divorce more likely and common, as if marriage were a contract that could be broken and renegotiated. As Pope Francis recently wrote:

> The family is experiencing a profound cultural crisis, as are all communities and social bonds.… Marriage now tends to be viewed as a form of mere emotional satisfaction that can be constructed in any way or modified at will. But the in-

dispensable contribution of marriage to society transcends the feelings and momentary needs of the couple. As the French bishops have taught, it is not born "of loving sentiment, ephemeral by definition, but from the depth of the obligation assumed by the spouses who accept to enter a total communion of life."[121]

Why the Church does not endorse so-called same-sex marriage

134. Premising marriage as mainly erotic or emotional satisfaction, which is a step made easier by the separation of sex and procreation, also enables arguments for same-sex unions. In some countries today there are movements to redefine marriage as if it could include *any* strong affective or sexual relationship between any consenting adults. Where divorce and contraception are established habits and this revised vision of marriage has taken root, redefining marriage to include same-sex marriage can seem a plausible next step.

135. With respect to the idea of same-sex marriage, as is well known, the Church declines to bless or sanction it. This does not imply any denigration or failure to appreciate the intensity of same-sex friendships and love. As should be clear at this point in this catechesis, the Catholic Church holds that everyone is called to give and receive love. Committed, sacrificial, chaste, same-sex friendships should be esteemed. Because Catholics are committed to love, hospitality, interdependence, and "bearing one another's burdens,"[122] the Church at all levels will want to nurture and support opportunities for chaste friendship, always seeking solidarity with those who, for whatever reason, are unable to marry.

136. True friendship is an ancient and honorable vocation. Saint Aelred of Rievaulx observed that the desire for a friend arises from

deep within the soul.[123] True friends produce a "fruit" and a "sweet-ness" as they help each other respond to God, encouraging one an-other in living the Gospel.[124] "Whether it develops between persons of the same or opposite sex, friendship represents a great good for all. It leads to spiritual communion."[125]

137. But, as should also be clear by now, when Catholics speak of marriage, we are referring to something distinct from other rela-tionships of particularly intense love, even if that love is deep and endures sacrificially and over long periods of time. Intense long-term affective intimacy is not sufficient for a marriage. Marriage, as indeed was universally recognized until very recently in the West, is premised on the duties arising from the possibilities and challenges posed by the procreative potential of a man and a woman.

138. The Church invites all men and women to see in their sexuality the possibility of a vocation. To reach maturity as a man or a woman means engaging certain questions to one's self: how is God calling me to integrate my sex into his plan for my life? Created in the image of God, our destiny is always communion, sacrifice, service, and love. The question for each and every one of us is how we will donate the sexual aspects of our lives in marriage or in celibate community. In neither case is our erotic desire or romantic preference sovereign or autonomous; in both cases, we will inevitably be called upon to make sacrifices which we would not choose if we were writing our own scripts.

The philosophical, legal, and political context for marriage today

139. Debates about redefining marriage, including questions of same-sex marriage, raise legal and political questions. In political theory and theology, Catholics speak of the family as a pre-political

institution.[126] To put it another way, the family is legally "antecedent" to civil society, the community, and the political state, since the family is "founded more immediately in nature."[127] Society does not invent or found the family; rather, the family is the foundation of society: "The family, in which the various generations come together and help one another grow wiser and harmonize personal rights with the other requirements of social life, is the very foundation of society."[128] Public authority thus has a duty to protect and serve the family.

140. Until recently, this view of the family was widely accepted by non-Catholics as well. The 1948 United Nations Universal Declaration of Human Rights insists that "the family is the natural and fundamental group unit of society and is entitled to protection by society and the State."[129] But as more jurisdictions re-imagine marriage as a matter of individual preference, dropping any organic connection to sexual difference and procreation, and promoting a contractual view of marriage, this consensus disappears. Today, the state purports more and more to invent marriage and redefine it at will.[130] Allegedly, the family no longer builds society and the state; rather, the state now presumes to supervise and license the family.

141. Some legislators are now trying to codify this philosophic reversal in new marriage laws. Instead of receiving marriage as an institution founded on nature, the new perspective regards marriage as infinitely plastic, as subordinate and malleable to political will. The Church has no choice but to resist this revisionism for the sake of protecting families, marriages, and children.

142. A society that mistakenly thinks marriage is always renegotiable, accountable only to self-referential human consent, will see marriage essentially as a contract, as a voluntary agreement between autonomous bearers of individual rights. But these mere contracts

LOVE IS OUR MISSION

are not the same as a marriage founded on a covenant of mercy. The logic of such contracts is not the Pauline logic of Ephesians 5, in which husbands and wives love one another in the manner of the Cross. The reasoning behind such defective contracts is at odds with the gift of marriage as a sacrament of the covenant.

143. The Church is obliged to resist the spread of false rationales for marriage. Pope Francis has observed:

> Again and again, the Church has acted as a mediator in finding solutions to problems affecting peace, social harmony, the land, the defense of life, human and civil rights, and so forth. And how much good has been done by Catholic schools and universities around the world! This is a good thing. Yet, we find it difficult to make people see that when we raise other questions less palatable to public opinion, we are doing so out of fidelity to precisely the same convictions about human dignity and the common good.[131]

144. As we said at the start of this catechesis, all of the Church's teachings about marriage, the family, and sexuality flow from Jesus. Catholic moral theology is a coherent narrative that satisfies humanity's deepest questions — a single, unified narrative flowing from basic Christian convictions about God's creation and covenant, humanity's fall, and Christ's incarnation, life, crucifixion, and resurrection. These teachings involve costs and suffering for all who would be Jesus' disciples, but they also open up new opportunities for beauty and human flourishing.

145. When the true nature of marriage is undermined or poorly understood, the family is weakened. When the family is weak, we are all prone to a type of brutal individualism. We too easily lose

the habit of Christ's gentleness and the discipline of his covenant. When the family is strong — when the family creates space for husbands, wives, and their children to practice the art of self-giving after the pattern of God's covenant — then light enters a dark world. In this light, the true nature of humanity can be seen. That is why the Church resists the shadows threatening the family.

146. *All of us are fallen. The disorder in each and every human heart has a social context and social consequences. The communion for which we were created is threatened by our disordered desires, our economic situations, by pornography, contraception, divorce, and legal or intellectual confusion. But love is our mission, and the Church seeks an alternative social life, a community premised on Jesus' mercy, generosity, freedom, and fidelity. The Church's many ministries further the culture of life, such aid to the poor, support for natural family planning, or articulating a more coherent philosophy for law. When Catholics resist divorce, or same-sex "marriage," or confused revisions to marital law, we also take responsibility for fostering communities of support and love.*

QUESTIONS FOR DISCUSSION

a) Explain the connections between the Church's care for the poor and the Church's teaching about sex and chastity.

b) What is the difference between contraception and natural namily planning?

c) What is the common denominator between divorce, contraception, and same-sex marriage?

d) What challenges to chastity exist in your community, and where should a person in your parish go to learn about the Church's perspective? How can your parish support people who want to live the Church's teachings?

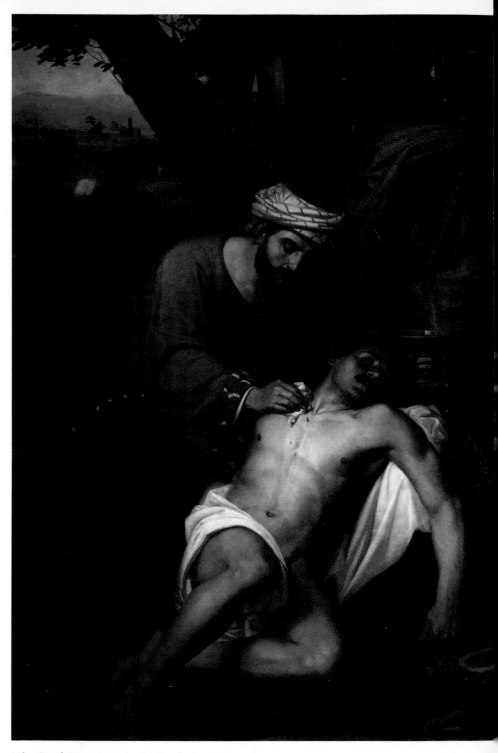

The Good Samaritan, José Manchola, 1852 / De Agostini Picture Library / G. Dagli Orti / Bridgeman Images

VIII. A HOME FOR THE WOUNDED HEART

Many people, especially today, face painful situations resulting from poverty, disability, illness and addictions, unemployment, and the loneliness of advanced age. But divorce and same-sex attraction impact the life of the family in especially intimate ways. Christian families and networks of families should be sources of mercy, safety, friendship, and support for those struggling with these issues.

Hearing the hard sayings of Jesus

147. Greeting the Holy Family in the Temple, Simeon declares that the child Jesus is destined "to be a sign that will be contradicted." (Lk 2:34, NAB) The Gospels prove the truth of these words in the reaction to Jesus' ministry by his contemporaries. Jesus offends even many of his own followers.[132] One reason is the "hard sayings" found in his words.

148. Some of Christ's hardest sayings deal with marriage, sexual desire, and the family. Jesus' teaching about the indissolubility of marriage shocks not only the Pharisees but his own followers: "If that is the case … it is better not to marry," murmur the disciples. (Mt 19:10) In the Sermon on the Mount, Jesus not only deepens the teaching of the Decalogue, but, as the New Moses, he calls his followers to a radical transformation of their hearts: "You have heard that it was said, 'You shall not commit adultery.' But I say to you,

everyone who looks at a woman in lust has already committed adultery with her in his heart." (Mt 5:27-28, NAB)

149. The Lord's disciples form a new messianic family that transcends and takes priority over traditional family relations.[133] For followers of the Christ, the water of Baptism is thicker than blood. The Lord's covenant gives a new context for understanding our bodies and our relations.

150. The Church continues the mission of Jesus in the world. "Whoever listens to you, listens to me," Jesus tells the disciples whom he sends out in his name. (Lk 10:16) The bishops, in communion with the Holy Father, succeed the apostles in their ministry.[134] Thus it should surprise no one that some Church teachings are also perceived as "hard sayings," out of step with current culture, especially on marriage, sexual expression, and the family.

The Church is a field hospital

151. To grasp the Church's ministry of teaching correctly, we also need to consider her pastoral nature. Pope Francis once famously likened the Church to "a field hospital after battle." He said: "It is useless to ask a seriously injured person if he has high cholesterol and about the level of his blood sugars! You have to heal his wounds. Then we can talk about everything else. Heal the wounds, heal the wounds.... And you have to start from the ground up."[135]

152. Sexuality is uniquely vulnerable to such wounds. Men, women, and children can be wounded by promiscuous sexual behavior (their own and that of others), pornography and other forms of objectification, rape, prostitution, human trafficking, divorce, and the fear of commitment created by an increasingly anti-marriage culture.[136] Because the family so deeply shapes its members — comprising

a "genealogy of the person" biologically, socially, and relationally — broken relationships within the family leave bitterly painful injuries.[137]

153. Pope Francis helps us to see the Church's "hard sayings" as words for our healing. But we need to engage in a kind of triage, treating the wounds according to their severity.

154. The Gospels are full of accounts of Jesus' healings. Christ the physician is a frequent image in the work of Saint Augustine. In an Easter homily he writes: "The Lord [like] an experienced doctor knew better what was going on in the sick man, than the sick man himself. Doctors do for the indispositions of bodies what the Lord can also do for the indisposition of souls."[138] Drawing on the parable of the Good Samaritan, Augustine sees the Church as the inn where the wounded traveler is taken to recover: "Let us, the wounded, entreat the physician, let us be carried to the inn to be healed … therefore Brothers, in this time the Church too, in which the wounded man is healed, is the inn of the traveler."[139]

155. In the Church, the first priority is to bring people to an encounter with the Divine Physician. Any encounter with Christ brings healing to fallen humanity, and the Holy Spirit can always be invited into our hearts to enable repentance and conversion. In the words of Pope Francis: "I invite all Christians, everywhere, at this very moment, to a renewed personal encounter with Jesus Christ, or at least an openness to letting him encounter them; I ask all of you to do this unfailingly each day. No one should think that this invitation is not meant for him or her, since 'no one is excluded from the joy brought by the Lord.'"[140]

156. When Pope Francis emphasized a personal encounter with Jesus, he reaffirmed the work of his predecessors. Pope Benedict XVI

said: "Being a Christian is not the result of an ethical choice or a lofty idea, but the encounter with an event, a person, which gives life a new horizon and a decisive direction."[141] And Pope John Paul II stressed that: *In order to make this 'encounter' with Christ possible, God willed his Church.* Indeed, the Church 'wishes to serve this single end: that each person may be able to find Christ, in order that Christ may walk with each person the path of life.'"[142]

157. The New Evangelization can be understood as bringing the wounded in from the battlefield of the world to encounter the Divine Physician and the healing that he offers within the community of the Church. Pope Francis sees this task as the challenge of being a "missionary Church," or "a Church which goes forth."[143]

With patience and forgiveness the Church helps us heal and grow

158. Within the Church, the healing power of God's grace is communicated by the Holy Spirit. The Holy Spirit makes Jesus present in the Church's liturgical worship, in her prayerful reading of Scripture in light of sacred tradition, and in her teaching office which is at the service of the Word of God.[144] Christ the Physician is particularly manifest in the Sacraments of Penance and Anointing the Sick, which are the two Sacraments of Healing.[145]

159. Taking part in sacramental life, developing a life of prayer, the practice of charity, spiritual disciplines, accountability and support from church friends — these things offer the wounded but recovering Christian a path of conversion. But conversion is not complete in an instant. It continues as a constant call for all members of the Church: "Christ's call to conversion continues to resound in the lives of Christians. This *second conversion* is an uninterrupted task for the

whole Church who, 'clasping sinners to her bosom, [is] at once holy and always in need of purification, [and] follows constantly the path of penance and renewal.'"[146]

160. The progressive nature of conversion shapes our ability to understand and live the Church's teaching. Speaking about the moral progress of married Christians Saint John Paul II distinguished between "the law of gradualness" and the "gradualness of the law."[147] The "law of gradualness" refers to the progressive nature of conversion. As they recover from the wounds of sin, Christians grow in holiness in every area of their lives, including their sexuality. When they fall short, they need to return to the mercy of God made accessible in the sacraments of the Church.

161. The "gradualness of the law," on the other hand, is the misleading idea that "different degrees or forms of precept in God's law [exist] for different individuals and situations."[148] For example, some wrongly argue that married couples who find Catholic teaching on responsible parenthood to be burdensome should be urged to follow their own consciences in choosing contraception. This is a false form of gradualism. It actually masks a kind of paternalism, denying the capacity of some members of the Church to respond to the fullness of God's love, and aiming to "lower the bar" of Christian moral teaching for them.

162. In a spirit of true gradualism, Pope Francis recently praised the courage of his predecessor Paul VI in his encyclical *Humanae Vitae*. In resisting growing social pressure for population control, Pope Francis said that Pope Paul's "genius was prophetic, he had the courage to side against the majority, defend moral discipline, put a brake on the culture, oppose neo-Malthusianism, present and future."[149]

163. But at the same time, Pope Francis noted that Paul VI told confessors to interpret his encyclical with "much mercy, [and] attention to concrete situations.... The question is not whether to change the doctrine, but to go deeper and make sure that pastoral care takes account of situations and of what each person is able to do."[150] Hence the Church calls her members to the fullness of the truth, and she encourages them to avail themselves of the mercy of God as they grow in their capacity to live it out.

Catholic teaching depends upon Catholic community

164. Many of Christ's moral teachings, and thus Catholic ethics, are demanding. But they presume in Christians a spirit of discipleship, a life of prayer, and a commitment to social and economic Christian witness. Above all, they presuppose life in a Christian *community* — i.e., a family of other men and women who have encountered Jesus, who together confess that he is Lord, wanting his grace to shape their lives, and helping each other respond to him.

165. Catholic teaching on homosexuality must be understood in that light. The same teaching that calls same-sex-attracted persons to lives of chastity in the form of continence calls *all* Catholics to abandon their own fears, to shun unjust discrimination, and to welcome their homosexual brothers and sisters to the communion of love and truth within the Church.[151] *All* Christians are called to face their disordered sexual inclinations and to grow in chastity — not a single human individual is untouched by this summons — and hence in their capacity to give and receive love in a manner consonant with their state in life.[152] Yet the response to this summons to conversion is inevitably a work in progress on the part of we recovering sinners who make up the Church's members. The key is to create within the family, the parish, and the wider Christian com-

munity an environment of mutual support where moral growth and change can occur.

166. Some of today's urgency to approve or give legal status to same-sex and opposite sex cohabitation comes from an understandable fear of loneliness. More and more in secular mainstream culture, having an erotic partner is perceived to be a necessity, and people think Church teaching is cruel, dooming men and women to a life of loneliness.

167. But if ordinary parishioners understood the rationale behind celibacy as a community practice, and if more domestic churches took the apostolate of hospitality more seriously, then the ancient Catholic teaching on chastity lived in continence outside of marriage might look more plausible to modern eyes. In other words, if our parishes really were places where "single" did not mean "lonely," where extended networks of friends and families really did share one another's joys and sorrows, then perhaps at least some of the world's objections to Catholic teaching might be disarmed. Catholics can embrace apostolates of hospitality no matter how hostile or indifferent the surrounding culture might be. Nobody is limiting lay or ordained Catholics in the friendship which we can offer those who struggle.

168. In her pastoral care of the divorced and remarried, the Church has sought to combine fidelity to Jesus' teaching on the indissolubility of marriage — which dismayed his disciples — with the mercy at the heart of his ministry. Consider, for example, Benedict XVI's teaching on the pastoral situation of divorced men and women:

> I see here a great task for a parish, a Catholic community, to do whatever is possible to help them to feel loved and

LOVE IS OUR MISSION

accepted, to feel that they are not "excluded."... This is very important, so that they see that they are accompanied and guided.... They need to realize that this suffering is not just a physical or psychological pain, but something that is experienced within the Church community for the sake of the great values of our faith. I am convinced that their suffering, if truly accepted from within, is a gift to the Church. They need to know this, to realize that this is their way of serving the Church; that they are in the heart of the Church.[153]

169. In other words, Pope Benedict presupposed the truth of what Christ taught, but he did not simply dismiss the divorced and remarried, telling them to grit their teeth or suffer in loneliness. That is not the Church's way, and any Catholic who acts as if it is should remember that one of the crimes of the Pharisees was burdening others with laws, yet not "lifting a finger" to help people with these burdens. (Mt 23:4) Rather, Benedict echoes the *Catechism of the Catholic Church*, which says "priests and the whole community must manifest an attentive solicitude" to divorced Catholics, so that they do not feel excluded.[154]

170. The bonds of friendship make the demands of discipleship bearable. "Bearing one another's burdens,"[155] within the Christian community, enables its members to walk a path of healing and conversion. Fraternal charity makes fidelity possible. It also offers a witness and encouragement to the wider Church. The *Catechism of the Catholic Church* has something like this in mind when it says spouses who persevere in difficult marriages "deserve the gratitude and support of the ecclesial community."[156] The same should be said for all who find themselves in challenging family situations.

171. In a culture that swings between anonymity on the one hand and voyeuristic curiosity "about the details of other people's lives" on the other, Pope Francis calls us to accompany each other in the work of spiritual growth.[157] He says: "Someone good at accompaniment does not give in to frustrations or fears. He or she invites others to let themselves be healed, to take up their mat, embrace the cross, leave all behind and go forth ever anew to proclaim the Gospel."[158] Those being healed are thus able to extend the invitation of healing to others.

172. Christian faith and the salvation it mediates are not individualistic; they are deeply communal: "Faith is necessarily ecclesial; it is professed from within the body of Christ as a concrete communion of believers. It is against this ecclesial backdrop that faith opens the individual Christian toward all others. Christ's word, once heard, by virtue of its inner power at work in the heart of the Christian, becomes a response, a spoken word, a profession of faith."[159]

173. *Jesus taught many things about sex and marriage which were difficult to live in both ancient times and today. But we are not alone as we face these difficulties. Life in the Body of Christ is meant to be lived as interdependent members, who build one another up in love.[160] The Church's teaching, sacraments, and community all exist to help us on the journey. With patience, forgiveness, and trust, in the Body of Christ, together we can heal and live in ways that might otherwise seem impossible.*

QUESTIONS FOR DISCUSSION ——————————————

a) The Church is a field hospital. How does the Church help people who are wounded? How can we do better?

b) Why aren't Catholics moral individualists? Why do we empha-
size the support of the community? How have you perceived
God's grace working through a community?

c) What are the obstacles to creating close spiritual friendships in
your culture? What can your parish or diocese do to encourage
Catholic friendships?

d) What support exists in your parish or diocese for making progress in chastity? Are there support groups or opportunities for
education? How often is the Sacrament of Penance offered, and
are there opportunities for spiritual direction?

Pentecost, Unknown Artist, 14th century / Church of St. Barbara, Cairo, Egypt, De Agostini Picture Library / G. Dagli Orti / Bridgeman Images

IX. MOTHER, TEACHER, FAMILY: THE NATURE AND ROLE OF THE CHURCH

The Church has institutional forms because she must work in the world. But that does not exhaust her essence. The Church is the Bride of Christ, a "she," not an "it." In the words of Saint John XXIII, she is our mother and teacher, our comforter and guide, our family of faith. Even when her people and leaders sin, we still need the Church's wisdom, sacraments, support, and proclamation of the truth, because she is the body of Jesus himself in the world — the family of God's people writ large.

The Church is our Mother; we are her sons and daughters

174. The Church is the heavenly Jerusalem, "that Jerusalem which is from above ... our Mother."[161] (Gal 4:26) The Church is the "mother of our new birth."[162] The Church, as Christ's Virgin Bride, gives birth to sons and daughters who are "born from above ... born of water and Spirit." (Jn 3:3,5, NAB)

175. What does it mean to be "born from above"? Does it mean we have no earthly identity after Baptism? No, but it does mean that "from the baptismal fonts is born the one People of God of the New Covenant, which transcends all the natural limits of nations, cultures, races, and sexes: 'For by one Spirit we were all baptized into one body.'"[163] It means that as sons and daughters of the Church we

have a new identity that does not destroy, but transcends, all of the ways in which human beings naturally construct their identities.

176. As members of the Church, we are members of the "one body" that is not defined by any human qualification, such as age, nationality, or intelligence, or by any human achievement, such as efficiency, organization, or moral virtue. If the Church were defined by any of these human qualities, we would have no rebirth "from above," but only from here below, from ourselves and our own limited abilities. For no matter how intelligent or virtuous we are, it is nothing compared to the perfect love of Christ, and his Bride, the Jerusalem from above, our Mother, the Church. In becoming her son or daughter, we are receiving a gift, a new identity in Christ, which we cannot give ourselves.

How and why the Church is holy

177. When we say that the Church is "immaculate," we do not ignore that all of her members are sinful, for the Church is "at once holy and always in need of purification."[164] Her holiness is the holiness of Christ, her Spouse. It is the love of Christ, the Bridegroom, that creates the Church in the first place: "The Church is born primarily of Christ's total self-giving for our salvation, anticipated in the institution of the Eucharist and fulfilled on the cross…. As Eve was formed from the sleeping Adam's side, so the Church was born from the pierced heart of Christ hanging dead on the cross."[165]

178. We could say that the "constitution" of the Church is not any virtue, holiness, or achievement we may have attained, but the self-giving love of Christ. When we are born of the Church as of our Mother, we are born of this love of Christ. This love gives the Church her identity, not as one nation or grouping or club humanly

constituted among others, but as the "Bride," the "Spouse," who is "one flesh" with Christ, and so one Body.

179. This love in which we are born in Christ is a love we cannot give ourselves. Once received, it is purifying, so that the Church, in the person of each of her sons and daughters, is always being transformed in Christ's love until Christ is fully formed in all of us. This is the meaning of the image of the pilgrim Church, a Church "on pilgrimage" toward her final perfection, perfection in and by the very love that defines her in the first place.

180. Until that time, the Church will find that her pilgrimage is one of constantly "following the path of penance and renewal,"[166] and she cannot, and does not, claim perfection except in her dowry, the blood of Christ, that is, his love.

When Catholics sin, it does not erase what is holy about the Church

181. The Church's basis in Christ means that sin in the Church, even sin in her ordained ministers, cannot invalidate the identity of the Church or her holiness, because the identity of the Church does not come from any of us. It comes from Christ. In the Old Testament, the people of God, Israel, were defined by their covenant with God, and no amount of sin on their part could invalidate that "chosenness" or the identity it gave them as the people of God. Wherever they went, God did not abandon them. Whoever encountered them always encountered the people of God, no matter how sinful any of the members of the people may have been.

182. God's covenant fidelity applies also to the Church. The miracle of the Church is that the love of Christ that defines her cannot be erased by any sin of her members. She is a visible society in the

world, but one that is not defined by anything that is "of" the world. That is what is so beautiful about the Church. We do not have to wait for the society of twelve perfect people to be created before we can declare we have a Church worth believing in. We do not place our faith in human virtues or perfections, but we believe in Jesus Christ, who died for us, and by his blood made us "a chosen race, a royal priesthood, a holy nation," God's own people, that we may declare the wonderful deeds of him who called us out of darkness into his marvelous light. (1 Pet 2:9)

The Church's teaching authority and responsibility

183. The Church, as our Mother, imparting to us a new identity in the love and holiness in which she herself was formed, also has the responsibility of teaching us, of forming us ever more perfectly in the new identity we have received, not from the world, but "from above." There is no secular authority that can discharge this function because the identity the Church receives and then imparts does not come from the achievements of the world, as we have seen, but transcends them, perfecting them all. Rather, "the pastoral duty of the Magisterium," or teaching authority of the Church, "is aimed at seeing to it that the People of God abides in the truth that liberates."[167]

184. The teaching authority of the Church serves the whole people of God by preserving the truth of the Gospel intact, together with all of the moral teachings revealed, explicitly and implicitly, in the Gospel, which nurture human freedom. These include such truths as the dignity of human persons, the goodness of creation, the nobility of the married state and its intrinsic orientation toward a life-giving communion of love. These truths cannot be annulled by sins committed against the dignity they proclaim. Rather, such sins call the Church to proclaim these truths ever more faithfully, even as she seeks renewal in these very truths, and in the love from which they come.

How married couples and families carry out the Church's witness

185. Christian spouses have the key role in proclaiming these very truths, in terms that the world finds most persuasive — that is, in lives that are continually transformed by the love that is imparted to couples in the Sacrament of Marriage and defines their communion as husband and wife. Pope Francis has described in a stirring way the witness to truth that Christian spouses can provide, supported by the graces of the Sacrament of Matrimony:

> Christian spouses are not naïve; they know life's problems and temptations. But they are not afraid to be responsible before God and before society. They do not run away, they do not hide, they do not shirk the mission of forming a family and bringing children into the world. But today, Father, it is difficult.... Of course it is difficult! That is why we need the grace, the grace that comes from the sacrament! The sacraments are not decorations in life — what a beautiful marriage, what a beautiful ceremony, what a beautiful banquet.... But that is not the Sacrament of Marriage. That is a decoration! Grace is not given to decorate life but rather to make us strong in life, giving us courage to go forwards! And without isolating oneself but always staying together, Christians celebrate the Sacrament of Marriage because they know they need it![168]

186. Popes John Paul II and Benedict XVI both had occasion to quote a passage from Paul VI's apostolic exhortation *Evangelii Nuntiandi:* "Modern man listens more willingly to witnesses than to teachers, and if he does listen to teachers, it is because they are witnesses."[169] Pope Francis is calling Christian spouses to be the kind of teachers that contemporary people listen to, teachers who teach by

their witness, and thereby uphold the truth and display its persuasiveness in their openness to new life, in the warmth of their mutual love and in the readiness of their hospitality, as oases of love and mercy in a culture so often marked by cynicism, hardheartedness, and discouragement.

187. The witness of Christian spouses can bring light into a world that has come to value efficiency over persons, and "having" over "being" — and thus has forgotten the value of "persons" and of "being" altogether. May those married in Christ be faithful witnesses to his love, and so become teachers of the truth, which is always and everywhere intrinsically compelling.

188. *The Church is an institution, but she is always more than an institution. She is a mother, a bride, a body, a family, and a covenant. All the baptized are her sons and daughters, giving Christians our most fundamental and authentic identity. Just as our own sinfulness never erases our creation in God's image and our membership in God's family, when Catholics sin, that does not erase the Church's holiness. The Church's essence depends on Jesus, a foundation which holds us accountable, but which is also deeper and more secure than any human achievement or failure. Despite her many failures, the Church cannot shirk the responsibility to preach the Gospel, and so we carry forward her mission of love.*

QUESTIONS FOR DISCUSSION ———————

a) How does God's covenant protect us, even when we sin?

b) Everyone sins, including Catholic leaders. Why do we say that the Church is holy anyway?

c) What does Jesus want us to do when the Church fails to live up to his standards?

d) Why does Jesus love the Church? What about the Church pleases him? What disappoints him?

Circle of Love / © 2014 Michael Escoffery / Artists Rights Society (ARS), New York. Photo: Michael Escoffery / Art Resource, NY

X. CHOOSING LIFE

God made us for a reason. His love is our life mission. This mission enables us to find our true identity. If we choose to embrace this mission, we will have a new perspective on many issues, not just the family. To live the mission of the domestic church means that Catholic families will sometimes live as minorities, with different values from their surrounding culture. Our mission of love will require courage and fortitude. Jesus is calling, and we can respond, choosing lives of faith, hope, charity, joy, service, and mission.

Our mission for the whole of life

189. We began this catechesis by explaining that God made us for a reason. The God we meet in Jesus Christ loves us, and calls us to love as he does. If we understand that love is our mission in our marriages, our families, our children, and our parishes, then we have learned a basic truth that will shape many other areas of life.

190. For example, if fidelity to the covenant requires restraint, if our bodies and the material world can be vessels of divine grace, then we can approach questions of ecology, technology, and medicine with a renewed humility. Similarly, if we follow God's commitment to a covenant love stronger than suffering, then we have new reasons for standing in solidarity with others who grieve or hurt. If we understand that the image of God, and therefore human dignity, is more

deeply rooted than any contingent human skill or achievement, then we can understand why the Church has so much love for the very young, the elderly, the disabled, and all those who will always depend upon others for basic care.

191. We now realize why a catechesis on the family has actually been a catechesis for all of life. As Pope Francis says, "Preaching the Gospel, in fact, is done first inside the family, and then in the different spheres of everyday life."[170] If we have learned to think of our families as domestic churches, if we have learned why moral individualism is not the right context for receiving Catholic teaching, then we have adopted a view that will reorient our whole identity.

Living as a creative minority

192. Catholic perspectives on the meaning of life and how to live well will not persuade everyone in this age. The era of "Christendom," when westerners could assume at least some sort of rough congruence between public values and Catholic values, is fading. Western post-Christendom Catholics are learning to live like Christians in many other parts of the world, places in Africa or Asia, where Christians have never been in the majority.

193. Minority status in a culture does not mean marginal or irrelevant status. The *Catechism of the Catholic Church*, teaching on our vocation to participate in society, cites a Christian letter, written at a time when the Church was far from established or socially prestigious. The temptation to withdraw must have been real, but the letter says: "Do not live entirely isolated, having retreated into yourselves as if you were already justified, but gather instead to seek the common good together."[171] This outward-looking, service-oriented spirit actually has an even more ancient pedigree. Said the prophet Jeremiah to the Jewish exiles in Babylon, even though the

Babylonians had sacked Jerusalem and taken the Jews prisoners: "Seek the welfare of the city to which I have exiled you; pray for it to the Lord, for upon its welfare your own depends." (Jer 29:7, NAB)

194. Living in the world as a creative, faithful minority takes spiritual discipline. In the Book of Daniel, Daniel and his Jewish friends are able to serve in the court of the Babylonian King Nebuchadnezzar. That Jews would go so far as to serve a pagan king is itself striking. But they were helpful to the king precisely insofar as they remained faithful Jews.

195. The reason that they had the wisdom which the King's magicians did not possess was that they had conformed their lives to faith in the one true God. They said their prayers[172] and maintained key Jewish disciplines (such as dietary restrictions[173]). They were leaven in a pagan palace because they knew who they were. They knew how to be in a particular social world but not of it. And they knew when not to compromise — they knew that their religious identity would sometimes be costly — and they accepted the lions' den and the fiery furnace rather than betray their God and worship idols.

196. Catholics, then, have strategies and precedents for living the faith in a world which does not understand their beliefs or agree with them. If our way of life is different from the world's, we nevertheless have a firm hope and a clear mind, "a plan bigger than our own ideas and undertakings, a plan which sustains us and enables us to surrender our future entirely to the one we love."[174] We have a firm foundation for independence from destructive forces in society and culture, and it is this same foundation which orients us to love and participation in society and culture. The "love which moves the sun and the other stars,"[175] the love which created and sustains all that is, is the same love which animates our marriages, our families,

our homes, and our Church. We can be confident that if we follow this love, even to the foot of the cross, our sufferings are actually making us more real, more authentically human, and that resurrection and vindication are coming, because we are following a trustworthy Lord. This love will give us the fortitude to live distinctively, as salt of the earth.[176]

We are all missionaries

197. Saint John Paul II exhorted, "Family, become what you are,"[177] and his words have lost nothing of their vibrancy; their urgency has only intensified in the face of the many challenges that families experience today. John Paul's insight was that the mission of the family flows from its identity in God's plan. "And since in God's plan it has been established as an 'intimate community of life and love,' the family has the mission to become more and more what it is, that is to say, a community of life and love in an effort that will find fulfillment ... in the kingdom of God."[178] In the words of John Paul II, the fundamental mission of the family therefore is "to guard, reveal, and communicate love," a mission that is "a living reflection of and a real sharing in God's love for humanity and the love of Christ the Lord for the Church, his Bride."[179] When the family embraces its missionary identity, the family becomes what it was always meant to become.

198. This mission is not reserved for the few or for the extraordinary. Nor does it mean that families somehow have to stop being themselves or seek after some impossible perfection in order to witness to the Gospel. The Christian family is called to deepen, reflect upon, and witness to the love and life that are already basic to being a family.

199. The family is a communion of love, founded upon the gift of self in the two-in-one-flesh communion of persons of husband and wife.

It is this indissoluble communion of husband and wife that sets the stage for the entire family as a true community of persons.[180] It is in the family that love is learned as a gift of self, a gift first received by the child from the father and mother and then given back and shared with others. The family is the place where the value of community is learned, forming the basis for communion in society. In this way, marriages and families that strive to love in unity and fidelity offer a vital witness in their homes, neighborhoods, parishes, local communities, and wherever they go, whether in service, work, or play.

The domestic church will find its fulfillment in the mission to the universal Church

200. The Church has never been far from the family home. Christ himself was born, raised, and formed "in the bosom of the holy family of Joseph and Mary."[181] Mary, as virgin and as mother, uniquely and beautifully recapitulates both the vocation to celibacy and the vocation to motherhood.[182] In their life together, the Holy Family of Nazareth is an example and intercessor for all families. During his own public ministry, Jesus would frequently visit or stay in the homes of families, especially the family of Saint Peter in Capernaum.[183] Saint Paul, in his greetings, would also acknowledge particular disciples, especially the couple Prisca and Aquila, and the "church at their house."[184] As the *Catechism of the Catholic Church* teaches:

> From the beginning, the core of the Church was often constituted by those who had become believers "together with all [their] household." When they were converted, they desired that "their whole household" should also be saved. These families who became believers were islands of Christian life in an unbelieving world.[185]

201. To speak of the family as a domestic church means that what is said of the Church herself can often be said analogously of the Christian family, and that the Christian family therefore plays a key role within the Church and the world. Pope John Paul II spoke of the "specific and original ecclesial role" of the Christian family: "The Christian family is called upon to take part actively and responsibly in the mission of the Church in a way that is original and specific by placing itself in what it is and what it does as an 'intimate community of life and love' at the service of the Church and of society."[186]

202. The Compendium of the *Catechism of the Catholic Church* describes the Sacrament of Marriage, along with that of Holy Orders, as "at the service of communion and mission."[187] Marriage and the family serve and build the communion of the Church and contribute to and advance her mission to proclaim the Gospel and to love as Christ has loved. Sometimes there can be a tendency to think solely of how the Church (and how one's particular diocese and parish) serves marriages and families. Indeed this is a vital part of the Church's pastoral outreach.

203. But just as important, and perhaps even more urgent, is to think of how the Christian family loves and serves the parish, the diocese, the universal Church, and the world. Ministry aimed to assist families should help them in turn become missionaries themselves. This is, in a certain sense, a paradigm shift that awaits full flowering in the Church: the unleashing of the Christian family for the work of advancing the Gospel. At the root of this is nothing other than a rediscovery of the vocation of marriage as a vocation to become a domestic church.

204. The domestic church is not an abstract concept. It is a reality, a vocation, and a mission, founded on the Sacrament of Marriage,

and being lived by many. Christ is still calling: Christian families, the Church needs you; the world needs you.

205. *Family, become what you are.*[188] *Choose life, then, that you and your descendants may live, by loving the Lord, your God, obeying his voice, and holding fast to him.*[189] *This mission will sometimes mark you as different from others in your society. To live your witness of love will require spiritual commitment and discipline, but do not fear. The Church is with you. The Lord is with you. The Lord has made a covenant with you. The Lord is calling. He will be faithful, and your covenant will bear fruit. Love is your mission, the basis for all communion, a profound adventure in service, beauty, and truth.*

QUESTIONS FOR DISCUSSION

a) In what way is a catechesis on the family actually a catechesis for the whole of life? In what ways do Catholic teachings about human nature, sex, marriage, and the family connect with other aspects of life?

b) Do the values and habits in your community make it easier or harder to be Catholic? In your culture, are you free to be fully Catholic, or is there pressure to compromise the faith? How can you participate in your culture while remaining faithful?

c) Does your family think of itself as a domestic church? What values are visible in the way your household lives? What steps can you take to be better missionaries?

d) What support does your family need from the Church? How can the Church help you? How can you help the Church and other families?

A PRAYER FOR THE WORLD MEETING OF FAMILIES IN PHILADELPHIA IN 2015

God and Father of us all,
in Jesus, your Son and our Savior,
you have made us
your sons and daughters
in the family of the Church.
May your grace and love
help our families
in every part of the world
be united to one another
in fidelity to the Gospel.
May the example of the Holy Family,
with the aid of your Holy Spirit,
guide all families, especially those most troubled,
to be homes of communion and prayer
and to always seek your truth and live in your love.
Through Christ our Lord. Amen.

Jesus, Mary and Joseph, pray for us!

ABBREVIATIONS USED IN THIS DOCUMENT

CCC, Catechism of the Catholic Church
CCCC, Compendium of the Catechism of the Catholic Church
CIC, Code of Canon Law
CSDC, Compendium of the Social Doctrine of the Church
CV, *Caritas in Veritate*
DCE, *Deus Caritas Est*
DD, *Dies Domini*
DV, *Dei Verbum*
EG, *Evangelii Gaudium*
EN, *Evangelii Nuntiandi*
FC, *Familiaris Consortio*
GS, *Gaudium et Spes*
GrS, *Gratissimam Sane*
HV, *Humanae Vitae*
LF, *Lumen Fidei*
LG, *Lumen Gentium*
MD, *Mulieris Dignitatem*
NAB, New American Bible
NMI, *Novo Millennio Ineunte*
NRSV, New Revised Standard Version (Bible)
PP, *Populorum Progressio*
RH, *Redemptor Hominis*
RN, *Rerum Novarum*

SC, *Sacramentum Caritatis*
ToB, Theology of the Body
VS, *Veritatis Splendor*
Books of the Bible are abbreviated as per the CCC

END NOTES

1. Cf. *Catechism of the Catholic Church* (CCC) (1992), 425-427.
2. Pope Francis, Encyclical *Lumen Fidei* (LF) (2013), 52.
3. Cf. LF, 57.
4. Pope John Paul II, Encyclical *Redemptor Hominis* (RH) (1979), 9.
5. CCC, 426.
6. LF, 57. Cf. Heb 12:2.
7. Vatican Council II, Pastoral Constitution *Gaudium et Spes* (GS) (1965), 22.
8. GS, 19.
9. Benedict XVI, "Eucharistic Celebration: Homily," 7th World Meeting of Families, Milan, June 2, 2012.
10. CCC, 2331.
11. Pope John Paul II, Apostolic Letter *Mulieris Dignitatem* (MD) (1988), 7.
12. MD, 7.
13. GS, 19.
14. RH, 10.
15. Cf. Gen 1:26-27, 2:24.
16. Pope John Paul II, Apostolic Exhortation *Familiaris Consortio* (FC) (1981), 11. Cf. Gen 1:26-27, 1 Jn 4:8, and GS, 12.
17. Pope Benedict XVI, Encyclical *Deus Caritas Est* (DCE) (2005), 11.
18. Cf. also Mt 15:32-39, Mk 6:31-44 and 8:1-9, Lk 9:10-17, and Jn 6:5-15.
19. Pope Benedict XVI, "Address...to participants in the forum of family associations," Rome (May 16, 2008).
20. DCE, 11.
21. Joseph Ratzinger, *In the Beginning: a Catholic understanding of the story of creation and fall* (Grand Rapids, MI: Wm. B. Eerdmans Publishing Co., 1995), 30.
22. DCE, 9.
23. Cf. Ezek 23.
24. Cf. Isa 50:1, 54:5, 61:10, 62:5.
25. Cf. Jer 2:2, 3:1, 3:6-12, 31:32.

26. Ps 45.

27. DCE, 9.

28. Cf. Ex 34:16, Judg 2:17, Num 15:39, and Deut 31:16.

29. Pope Francis, Homily, "The Pope's Mass at Santa Marta - When a love fails," *L'Osservatore Romano* (February 28, 2014).

30. DCE, 5.

31. Eph 5:21-33.

32. DCE, 12. Cf. Jn 19:37 and 1 Jn 4:8.

33. Cf. CCC, 1602. Cf. Rev 19:7,9 and Gen 1:26-27.

34. Saint Hildegard of Bingen, *Explanatio Symboli Sancti Athanasii* in *Patrologia Latina* 197, 1073. Cf. 1 Cor 6:19.

35. CCC, 2331, and FC, 11.

36. Pope Francis, Homily, "The Pope's Mass at Santa Marta - When a love fails," *L'Osservatore Romano* (February 28, 2014).

37. CCC, 362.

38. Pope John Paul II, Wednesday Audiences *Theology of the Body* (ToB) (January 9, 1980).

39. Congregation for the Doctrine of the Faith, Letter *On the Collaboration of Men and Women* (2004), 8.

40. Pope Paul VI, Encyclical *Humanae Vitae* (HV) (1968), 12.

41. CCC, 371.

42. CCC, 371.

43. Cf., ToB (January 2, 1980).

44. GS, 12.

45. Karol Wojtyla, *Love and Responsibility* (Ignatius Press, 1993), 171.

46. CCC, 2348-2349. Cf. St. Ambrose, *De viduis* 4.23.

47. CCC, 2349.

48. LF, 53.

49. Cf. ToB (January 16, 1980).

50. CCC, 1646.

51. CCC, 2391.

52. Pope Francis, Address "Meeting with the Young People of Umbria," Assisi (October 4, 2013).

53. Pope Francis, General Audience "Marriage, the heart of God's loving plan for humanity" (April 2, 2014).

54. Pope Francis, Address "Dialogue with Engaged Couples," Vatican City (February 14, 2014).

55. Pope Francis, Address "Dialogue with Engaged Couples," Vatican City (February 14, 2014).

56. CCC, 1642.

57. Pope Francis, Address "Dialogue with Engaged Couples," Vatican City (February 14, 2014).

58. CCC, 1615.

59. CCC, 1127.

60. CCC, 1617.

61. CIC, 1056-1057.

62. CIC, 1055.

63. GS, 47.

64. Saint Augustine, *De Bono Conjugali* 32; *De Genesi ad Litteram* 9.7.12; *De nuptiis et concupiscentia*, 1.10.11, 17.19, 21.23.

65. HV, 10.

66. CCC, 1652-1653. Cf. GS 48, 50.

67. Pope Francis, Homily "Feast of the Baptism of the Lord," Sistine Chapel (January 12, 2014).

68. Deut 6:4-7. Emphasis added.

69. FC, 14.

70. Vatican Council II, Dogmatic Constitution *Lumen Gentium* (LG) (1964), 11.

71. Saint Augustine, *The City of God Against the Pagans* (Cambridge, Cambridge University Press, 1998), p. 667, §15.16.

72. LG, 11. Cf. CCC, 1655-1658.

73. Pope Paul VI, Encyclical *Populorum Progressio* (PP) (1967), 15.

74. See above, ⁋60.

75. Pope Francis, Address "Meeting with the Young People of Umbria," Assisi (October 4, 2013).

76. Cf. Mt 6:10, 7:21, 12:50, 21:31, 26:39.

77. Saint Thérèse of Lisieux, *The Autobiography of Saint Thérèse of Lisieux: The Story of a Soul*, trans. John Beevers (Doubleday, 2001), 9.

78. GS, 38.

79. Pope Francis, Address "Meeting with the Clergy, Consecrated People and Members of Diocesan Pastoral Councils," Assisi (October 4, 2013).

80. CCC, 1656.

81. Cf. Jn 15:19 and Rom 12:2.

82. CCC, 1303, 1308

83. Pope Benedict XVI, Address "Families Teach Meaning of Life" (October 4, 2010).

84. Pope Benedict XVI, Address "Make Parish a Family of Families" (March 21, 2011).

85. Cf. FC, 44.

86. Cf. FC, 71, 77.

87. Pontifical Council for the Family, *Enchiridion of the Family* (2004), 1303-1304.

88. FC, 44.

89. Pope John Paul II, Address "Meeting of the adoptive families organized by the Missionaries of Charity" (September 5, 2000).

90. FC, 41.

91. Compendium of the Catechism of the Catholic Church (CCCC) (2005), 321.

92. Pope John Paul II, Address "Meeting of the adoptive families organized by the Missionaries of Charity" (September 5, 2000).

93. Cf. 1 Corinthians 7:25-40.

94. Pope Francis, Address, "Meeting with the Young People of Umbria," Assisi (October 4, 2013).

95. CCC, 2349. Cf. St. Ambrose, *De viduis* 4.23. Also, see above, ¶51.

96. CCC, 1646. See above, ¶58.

97. CCC, 2391. See above, ¶58.

98. See above, ¶60.

99. Cf. Lk 1:38.

100. CCC, 2347.

101. CCC, 2348.

102. CCC, 1624.

103. FC, 13.

104. Cf. John 1:14, 17:24.

105. CCC, 2344.

106. CCC, 1658.

107. CCC, 1658.

108. CCC, 1606.

109. Synod of Bishops, Extraordinary General Assembly, Preparatory Document "Pastoral Challenges to the Family in the Context of Evangelization," Vatican City (2013).

110. Pope Francis, Angelus, Vatican City (December 22, 2013).

111. Pope Benedict XVI, Encyclical *Caritas in Veritate* (CV) (2009), 15.

112. Pope Benedict XVI, Message "For the celebration of the world day of peace" (January 1, 2008).

113. Cf. Mt 2:13-23.

114. Pope Francis, Angelus, Vatican City (December 29, 2013).

115. Pope Pius XII, "Allocution to Midwives" (October 29, 1951).

116. Pope Pius XII, "Allocution to Midwives" (October 29, 1951).

117. Pope Francis, Angelus, Vatican City (December 22, 2013).

118. Pope Benedict XVI, Message "On the occasion of the 40th anniversary of Paul VI's encyclical *Humanae Vitae*" (October 2, 2008).

119. HV, 10. Cf. CCC, 2368. Also, see above, ¶72.

120. Cf. HV, 17.

121. EG, 66.

122. See above, ¶88.

123. Saint Aelred of Rievaulx, *De Spirituali Amicitia*, 1:51.

124. Saint Aelred of Rievaulx, *De Spirituali Amicitia*, 1:45-46.

125. CCC, 2347. See above, ¶102.

126. CSDC, 214.

127. Pope Leo XIII, Encyclical *Rerum Novarum* (RN) (1891), 13.

128. GS, 52.

129. UN Universal Declaration of Human Rights, Article 16.

130. Cf. EG, 66.

131. EG, 65.

132. Cf. Jn 6:60-66.

133. Cf. Mk 3:13-35 and Lk 8:19-21.

134. Cf. CCC, 77, 85. Cf. Dei Verbum (DV), 7.

135. Pope Francis, Interview Article "A Big Heart Open to God," *America* (September 30, 2013).

136. Cf. CCC, 2351-2356, and FC, 24.

137. Cf. Pope John Paul II, Letter to Families *Gratissimam Sane* (GrS) (1994), 9.

138. Saint Augustine, *Sermons*, 2290, *The Works of St. Augustine: A Translation for the 21ˢᵗ Century. Sermons* III/6 (184- 229Z), trans. Edmund Hill, O.P., ed. John Rotelle, O.S.A. (New York, 1993), 323. For other instances in which Augustine describes salvation in medical terms see *Serm*. 229E (*ibid.*, p. 283); *Confessions* VII, xx, 26; X, xxx, 42; *De doctrina christiana* 1, 27; 4, 95; *Enchiridion* 3.11; 22.81; 23. 92; 32.121; *De nuptiis*, Bk. 2, 9. III; 38. XXIII.

139. Saint Augustine, *Tractates on the Gospel of John*, 41.13.2. *Saint Augustine Tractates on the Gospel of John 28-54*, trans. John W. Rettig (Washington: CUA Press, 1993), 148-49.

140. EG, 3.

141. DCE, 1.

142. Pope John Paul II, Encyclical *Veritatis Splendor* (VS) (1993), 7.

143. EG, 19-24.

144. DV, 10.

145. CCC, 1421.

146. CCC, 1428. Cf. LG, 8.

147. FC, 34.

148. FC, 34.

149. Francis X. Rocca, "Pope, in interview, suggests…" Catholic News Service (March 5, 2014).

150. Francis X. Rocca, "Pope, in interview, suggests..." Catholic News Service (March 5, 2014).

151. Cf. CCC, 2358-2359.

152. Cf. CCC, 2337, 2348.

153. Pope Benedict XVI, Address "Evening of Witness", Milan (June 2, 2012).

154. CCC, 1651.

155. Gal 6:2. See above, ⁋88.

156. CCC, 1648.

157. EG, 169-73.

158. EG, 172.

159. LF, 22.

160. Cf. 1 Cor 12:26-27 and CCC, 521, 953.

161. Cf. CCC, 757.

162. CCC, 169.

163. CCC, 1267. Cf. 1 Cor 12:13.

164. LG, 8, and CCC, 827.

165. CCC, 766.

166. LG, 8, and CCC, 827.

167. CCC, 890.

168. Pope Francis, Address "To the participants in the pilgrimage of Families during the Year of Faith," Vatican City (October 26, 2013).

169. EN, 41.

170. Pope Francis, Angelus "Talk about the Holy Family as refugees" (December 29, 2013).

171. CCC, 1905.

172. Dan 6:11.

173. Dan 1:8.

174. LF, 52. See above, ⁋2.

175. Dante, *The Divine Comedy: Paradiso,* Canto XXXIII.

176. Cf. Mt 5:13.

177. FC, 17.

178. FC, 17. Cf. GS, 48.

179. FC, 17.

180. FC, 18-27.

181. CCC, 1655.

182. CCC, 507.

183. Cf. Mk 1:29-31, Mt 8:14-15, and Lk 4:38-39. Cf. Mk 2:1, 3:19-20, 7:17, 9:33. Cf. Mk 5:38, 7:24, 10:10, 14:3; Mt 9:23, 10:11-13, 13:1, 17:25, 26:6; Lk 5:29, 7:36, 8:51, 10:5-7, 11:37, 14:1, 19:5-9; and Jn 4:53, 12:1-2.

184. Rom 16:5 and 1 Cor 16:19. Cf. Col 4:15 and Phil 4:22.

185. CCC, 1655. Cf. Acts 18:8, 16:31, 11:14.
186. FC, 50.
187. CCCC, 321. See above, ¶91.
188. FC, 17.
189. Deut 30:19-20.